Working through Whiteness

Working through Whiteness

Examining White Racial Identity and Profession
with Pre-Service Teachers

Kenneth James Fasching-Varner

LEXINGTON BOOKS
Lanham • Boulder • New York • Toronto • Plymouth, UK

KH

Published by Lexington Books
A wholly owned subsidiary of The Rowman & Littlefield Publishing Group, Inc.
4501 Forbes Boulevard, Suite 200, Lanham, Maryland 20706
www.rowman.com

10 Thornbury Road, Plymouth PL6 7PP, United Kingdom

British Library Cataloguing in Publication Information Available

Library of Congress Cataloging-in-Publication Data
Library of Congress Cataloging-in-Publication Data Available
ISBN 978-0-7391-7686-3 (cloth : alk. paper)
ISBN 978-0-7391-7687-0 (electronic)

♾️™ The paper used in this publication meets the minimum requirements of American
National Standard for Information Sciences—Permanence of Paper for Printed Library
Materials, ANSI/NISO Z39.48-1992.

Printed in the United States of America

10/20/14

Dedication

To the nation's children, may we learn to serve you better.

Acknowledgments

I would like to acknowledge a number of significant people without whom this book would not have been possible.

Dr. Gloria Ladson-Billings and Dr. Adrienne Dixson, your models of scholarship have been significantly influential. Your work makes a difference in people's lives and I hope that one day my work might do the same.

The participants in this study shared honestly so that we may better understand how whiteness operates, and I am thankful that through their narratives we might better prepare future teachers to serve all children.

Ms. Martha Murray and Ms. Desiree Cho have been invaluable throughout the writing, editing, and production of this book. Marty has been an amazing friend and colleague over the last decade. Desiree has made a huge impact through her organization, attention to detail, and work ethic.

Mr. Eric Wrona of Lexington Books has been an incredible editor and thoughtful guide through this process. Eric believed in this book, supporting its development from the beginning. The entire Lexington staff has been incredibly supportive to make this book come to fruition.

To the children I taught in Rochester, New York, and to the children my students teach. Your futures inspire me to want to know better and do better.

I am thankful to my parents for their love and support. Without my parents none of this work would be possible.

Contents

Foreword: Primum Non Nocere, by Adrienne D. Dixson   ix

  1   Introduction   1
  2   Racial Identity and Pre-service Teachers   13
  3   Mapping the Terrain   29
  4   Semantic Moves Relative to Race   43
  5   Naïveté in Rationales for Being Teachers   71
  6   White Racial Identity   81
  7   Implications and Future Directions   115

Afterword: The Long Hard Look, by Roland W. Mitchell   125

Bibliography   131
Index   145
About the Author   147

Foreword
Primum Non Nocere:
Race, Identity and White Pre-service Teachers

By Adrienne D. Dixson

The Latin phrase *primum non nocere*, "first, do no harm," has particular meaning for those of us who study race and urban education and for scholars in multicultural teacher education. Although it would make sense to title this foreword, "Know Thyself," especially in light of the author's focus on White racial identity, I want to suggest that in the process of "knowing" themselves, White pre- and in-service teachers first commit themselves to not harming their students. At first blush, asking novice teachers to commit to not harming their students may seem out of place; however, we know that teachers' dysconsciousness about race, coupled with their beliefs about students' abilities based on other markers of difference, can have harmful effects on the educational success of their students (King, 1992; Rist, 2000; Rosenthal & Jacobsen, 1968). As I will discuss later, racialized harm has changed from physical violence through lynching to a more subtle, but no less violent form of psychological and emotional harm often done unintentionally through the racist beliefs and attitudes White teachers hold toward students of color. In this book, Kenneth Fasching-Varner helps us think about the ways to identify and address the potential "harm" caused by teachers' racial discourse.

Finding schools that educate *all* students has been an abiding issue in American public education since the historic *Brown v. Board of Education of Topeka, Kansas* decision in 1954. While the hope of the decision was that it would end racialized educational inequality, in the nearly fifty eight years since, educational inequity and racial segregation in American public education is even more entrenched and exacerbated. Concomitantly, most believed (and many still do) that *Brown* would essentially end racism in the United States. The belief then, and to a large extent now, especially with the election of the first African American president of the United States, was that desegregated schools would create racial harmony if nothing else because White children and Black children would "learn" through proximity, to get along with each other. Although some research suggests that racial attitudes have "improved," especially those of Whites towards other racial groups, sociologist Eduardo Bonilla-Silva (2004) suggests that perhaps the framing of this research obfuscates the ways that negative racial attitudes have merely become deeply entrenched in mainstream discourse. In essence, Bonilla-Silva argues that framing contemporary racial attitudes based on a racial discourse from the 1940s when racism was rampant and unabashed, fails to account for how people, especially Whites, have learned to mask overt racist attitudes because it is socially unacceptable and illegal in particular public institutions.

This masking of racist attitudes coupled with the belief that desegregated schools would radically change nearly a century of racial violence captures the challenge of current research on teacher education and teacher preparation. What was unaccounted for until much later in the post-*Brown* era was how teachers, specifically White teachers, might also harbor racist attitudes and beliefs about children of color and their families. Scholars in multicultural teacher education have focused on how to engage teachers not only in making curriculum more reflective of the multicultural/multiethnic society in the United States, but also to interrogate their racial beliefs and attitudes. The ultimate goal of research in this area is to positively impact teachers' pedagogies, particularly for teachers who work in classrooms with students of color.

While most of the multicultural teacher education research has examined curricula in schools and classrooms, teacher education programs and effective pedagogies, fewer studies have examined the racial discourses of teachers and pre-service teachers independent of their participation in specific multicultural and/or anti-racist courses and professional development seminars. That is, those studies that examine pre- and in-service teachers' racial beliefs and attitudes about multicultural curricula are generally examined within the context of the teachers' participation in a specific multicultural course or professional development seminar. The premise of the research and the courses is to "intervene" and/or transform White teachers' beliefs and attitudes about people of color and working in "diverse" contexts. Essentially, much of the research in this vein examines the effectiveness of the courses, immersion experiences or professional development seminars on changing teacher beliefs and/or impacting their pedagogies. What is often missing is the long-term impact of those beliefs and attitudes, and/or how a shift in attitude translates into their actual pedagogy. Yet, this research assumes that it is possible to design a single intervention and/or course that will undo nearly a lifetime of negative and indeed racist attitudes and beliefs about people of color. Moreover, this research assumes that White racial attitudes are uniform and will respond to "interventions" in a uniform manner. What is unknown, or at least not yet extensively researched, is what attitudes do pre-service teachers hold about race even after they have completed their teacher education programs and then as they are waiting to begin their new jobs as teachers? Moreover, we know very little about the ways in which White pre-service teachers engage in what Bonilla-Silva (2004) and other race scholars describe as "color-blind racism." That is, in what ways do White pre-service teachers engage in a discourse that, for all intents and purposes, appears to be race neutral and even liberal, yet upon closer examination is problematic for its potential impact on pedagogy and is inherently racist? Kenneth Fasching-Varner helps to expand our current thinking on preparing teachers for diverse class-rooms by looking more closely at the ways in which White pre-service teachers engage in racist thinking that is undisrupted by multicultural course work and diverse field placements. Moreover, Fasching-Varner's work in this book demonstrates the need for teacher education programs, and indeed most pro-grams that purport to prepare teachers for diverse contexts, to interrogate more rigorously new teachers' interests in and motives for going into the profession. To be clear, Fasching-Varner's work is not just a commentary on traditional teacher education programs. While his participants were from a traditional teacher education program, they represent the diversity among Whites who ar-ticulate an interest in teaching. That is, even alternative teacher preparation pro-grams should take heed of Fasching-Varner's research, perhaps even more closely than traditional programs, especially in light of the current political mo-ment where we see an all-out attack on schools and colleges of education and traditional teacher education programs in particular.

While Fasching-Varner's research shows that racist attitudes are deeply en-trenched, there is some hope, and Fasching-Varner's research suggests, that at least the new teachers have an awareness of difference and its relationship to pedagogy. In other words, teacher education matters in this area and can be even more effective in intervening and disrupting White teachers' racist attitudes and beliefs if structured and engaged in more meaningful ways. Thus, the attitudes and beliefs articulated by Fasching-Varner's participants are similar to those of young White college graduates who have an interest in and are selected for

Teach For America (The Real World, 2010), where little to no direct discussion about race, racism, and its impact on pedagogy occurs (Veltri, 2010). Hence, the implications of his research are significant if we take seriously what it means to prepare teachers to truly teach *all* children. Fasching-Varner invites scholars in multicultural teacher education to engage pre-service teachers in substantive examinations of race and racism in their own discourse. While there is certainly more work to be done in this area, he provides us with a very important first step.

References

Bonilla-Silva, E. (2004). From bi-racial to tri-racial: Towards a new system of racial stratification in the USA. *Ethnic and Racial Studies, 27*, 931-950.

King, J. (1992). Dysconscious racism: Ideology, identity and the miseducation of teachers. *Journal of Negro Education, 60*, 133-146.

Rist, R. (2000). Student social class and teacher expectations: The self-fulfilling prophecy in ghetto education. *Harvard Education Review, 70*, 257-301.

Rosenthal, R., & Jacobson, L. (1968). *Pygmalion in the classroom.* New York, NY: Holt, Rinehart & Winston.

The Real World of Teach For America: The series. (2010). [Electronic source.] John Tulenko, David Wald, Valerie Visconti, Tania McKeown & Donald Devet (Producers). New York: PBS.

Veltri, B. (2010). *Learning on other people's children: Becoming a Teach For America teacher.* Charlotte, NC: Information Age Publishing.

Chapter 1
Introduction

SE wo were fin a wosankofa a yenkyi
It is not wrong to go back for that which you have forgotten.
African proverb

As you begin to read, I want to make visible both who I am and why I undertook the process of writing this text. I am a white teacher educator committed to issues of multiculturalism, social justice, and equitable education. I have taught at institutions of public and private higher education with student bodies of approximately 95+% white pre-service teachers. I have often found myself in the paradoxical situation of being a white male socialized to be white, yet believing that I work to disrupt the dominance of whiteness. My daily struggle was, and is, how to move white educators forward, including me, in a way that disrupts whiteness rather than masking or ignoring the power of whiteness. Children are taught both explicit and implicit lessons about whiteness from teachers, highlighting the importance of disrupting whiteness' privileged status. It is these lessons that are taught to children about race that bring me to studying how pre-service teachers understand the work they do as well as their sense of what their white racial identity might be.

Over the past eight years, I have interacted with approximately five hundred teacher candidates in teaching multiculturalism and diversity courses at the graduate and undergraduate levels. An often-repeated refrain from candidates is, "Tell me how to teach _____ students," whereas the desire is most often to learn about how to deal with "others" as opposed to self. In my teaching, I continually and consciously attempt to balance my own personal narrative of being both white and male, the most dominant and oppressive group in the landscape of the United States, while pushing for teachers to challenge their own whiteness and the benefits we reap as white people. In balancing who I am with what I believe about teaching and preparing teacher educators, I am struck by the resistance many white educators exhibit when asked to pivot the focus from how to work with others to a focus on how to learn about self. Resistance comes from many

1

angles; pre-service teachers often attempt to represent an explicitly politically correct, progressive, and evolved view of difference while inserting "buts" and "wells" that serve to embed a more implicit perspective on those who the teacher candidates believe are not like them.

Teacher educators can learn both about white racial identity development and how a teacher's sense of whiteness informs pedagogical beliefs from the narratives of white pre-service teachers. Narratives, moreover, provide insight into how teachers serve as agents of socialization to students from both marginalized and dominant groups. Narratives have the potential to help us understand the ways in which teachers' beliefs about race perpetuate racial stratification and maintain white supremacy through the socializing nature of public education. This book will not only provide a detailed exploration of white racial identity development as seen through the lens of a group of pre-service educators, but the book also provides a challenge to current modes of thinking about white racial identity that are framed in purely developmental ways.

The Demographic Problem of Race and Education

According to the Pew Center for Research (Fry, 2007), 74% of white students attend schools where less than 5% of students come from historically underrepresented groups such as Black/African American or Latino/a. Nearly 60% of students from historically underrepresented groups attend schools that are defined as "all or nearly all minority," whereby less than 5% of the student body is white (Fry, 2007). Teacher demographics provide an equally disturbing perspective: the National Center for Education Information (2005) estimates that over the last twenty years, 85% to 92% of the teaching force is white.

The explicit messages derived from these statistics about students and teachers is that students in the United States receive increasingly stratified and segregated learning experiences while being taught by a predominance of white teachers, most of whom likely were educated in racially segregated settings themselves. Inherent to these messages is the idea that white people continue to have the opportunity to socialize white, black, and brown students. Through varied foci, researchers have explored the effects, implications, and contradictions of a schooling system dominated and overseen by white educators (Carter & Goodwin, 1994; Haviland, 2008; Hernandez Sheets, 2001; Ladson-Billings, 2006a; Sleeter, 2001, 2005). Rodgers, Marshall, and Tyson (2006) and Ball (2002) have explored the narratives inherent to the claim of preparing teachers for "diverse settings" and "at risk students" respectively. Gee (2001) and Cook-Gumperz (1993) are among scholars who have looked at the importance of identity with respect to education and educational research. Finally, sociologist Bonilla-Silva (2003, 2006) has examined the impact of racism in general, whereas education scholars DeCuir and Dixson (2004) have examined the impact of racism with a focus on education.

The intersectional nature of the above scholarship and the racialized makeup of the teaching force suggest four questions regarding teacher educators. First, to what extent are white educators' racial narratives problematic? Second, how do narratives of pre-service teachers inform said pre-service teachers' pedagogical beliefs? Third, to what extent do teachers understand the nature of why they enter the profession? And, finally, what do the narratives and understandings of vocation reveal both about the public and private articulation of the teachers' own white racial identity and consequently pedagogical practices? These questions have implications for not only teacher education but also for how we understand the perpetuation of the achievement gaps in education (Ladson-Billings, 2006b).

Purpose of the Study

It is important at the outset of this book to share the purposes for studying the pre-service teachers who influenced the study later in the book that provides the basis for exploring racial identity and vocation. The overall purposes of the study were to examine the racial narratives of white pre-service educators, to contribute to the scholarly writing on whiteness, and to examine the effects of whiteness in education. Inherent in the purposes was my desire to examine white teachers' presentations of their white racial narratives and the white racial identity expressed within said identities. This study was premised on three interrelated notions about race and, more specifically, on white people's conceptions of and experiences with race.

The first premise is that white teachers make up a significant portion of the teaching force in the United States, thus any effort at reforming the performance of students must trace back to the teachers who both educate and socialize the nation's student body. Attention has been paid to the idea of the achievement gap for United States students (Ladson-Billings, 2006b). Ladson-Billings (2006b) proposed the idea of debt as a mechanism to understand the long-term and systemic nature of the achievement gap and educational disparity. I argue that the unexamined racial narratives, and, consequently, unexamined nature of white racial identity development for teachers, contribute to the historical, sociopolitical, and moral educational debts that Ladson-Billings (2006b) discusses. She has argued that educational debts work in tandem with economic debts to create inequity in our nation's public schools. As such, redressing the achievement gap might begin with an examination of white teacher narratives, the first purpose of the study.

Second, with teachers serving as one of the primary socializing forces in students' lives, the teacher's racialized identity is an important component to better understanding how students become socialized to beliefs about race. Woods and Demerath (2001) suggest that teaching is an "act of persuasion," and, if this proposition is true, the act of persuasion is necessarily steeped in the identity(ies) of the teachers themselves. A rigorous study of the narratives of white teachers appears as one way to address how the pedagogical beliefs and practices of teachers are shaped. Gay (1984) suggests that there are implications of identity development for educators and that those implications would be embedded in the narratives of teachers (Gee, 2001; Cook-Gumperz, 1993).

The third purpose of conducting this research relates to the value of the narratives themselves. Critical race theorists (Bell, 1995a, 1995b; Crenshaw, 1995; Delgado, 1989, 1990; Delgado & Stefanic, 1997, 2001; Dixson & Rousseau, 2005; Harris, 1995; Fasching-Varner, 2009; Ladson-Billings & Tate, 1995) suggest that whiteness holds certain value as property. Given the nature of whiteness as property, the narratives of white people have the potential of serving as instruments that denote value. Thus, how does the narrative, or the value of whiteness, socialize children to the meaning of whiteness? More importantly, how are narratives negotiated into the pedagogical practices of teachers? An understanding of how white educators link the value of whiteness, as exhibited in their narratives, to their ideas about teaching and learning can give teacher educators considerable insight into addressing the preparation of teachers, and how teacher educators might approach dismantling whiteness' deleterious effects.

The purposes of this study link to Sankofa, or the Asanta Adink, a notion of go back and take (Grayson, 2000). In her keynote presidential address to the American Educational Research Association, Ladson-Billings (2006b) suggested that much effort in education is spent on programs and ideas to service a so-called achievement gap between students of color and non-students of color in the United States. Ladson-Billings highlighted that such efforts are akin to paying interest on debt—one makes continual payment to servicing interest but the principle is never redressed. The research presented in this book reflects both on my narrative as a white educator and the narratives of white pre-service teachers in an attempt to gain clarity on what informs the worldviews and identities of white teachers. To move forward in redressing educational inequity, teacher educators must understand the racial narratives of teacher candidates to prepare them to recognize and to disrupt the totalizing effects that teacher narratives have on pedagogical beliefs. Delgado (1989) argues that it is critically important for white people to understand their own racial narratives as they often serve as the basis for what we do with/to others.

Theoretical Frameworks

This work in this book is informed both by Critical Race Theory (CRT) and White Racial Identity Theory (WRIT). As such, I provide the theoretical frameworks of CRT and WRIT early in the text, since both areas of theoretical introspection shaped the direction of the study and inform the analyses throughout this book.

Critical Race Theory

Since Ladson-Billings and Tate (1995) introduced CRT to the field of education, a number of education scholars and researchers have used CRT to analyze the ways in which race impacts educational outcomes and opportunities (DeCuir & Dixson, 2004; Delgado Bernal & Villapando, 2002; Dixson & Rousseau, 2005; Duncan, 2006; Fasching-Varner, 2009; Ladson-Billings & Tate, 1995; Solórzano & Yosso, 2002; Tate, 1994, 1997; Tate & Rousseau, 2002; Taylor, 2000). Three concepts steeped in CRT are useful as theoretical lenses by which to explore the narratives of white educators; (counter)storytelling, whiteness as property, and expansive/restrictive views of racism.

(Counter)stories
(Counter)story telling is an important aspect of Critical Race Theory (DeCuir & Dixson, 2004; Delgado, 1989, 1990; Dixson & Rousseau, 2005; Ladson-Billings, 2005; Solórzano & Yosso, 2002). Counterstories serve to counteract the stories of the dominant group, providing scholars with both a voice and a structure to interrupt irrational discourses about race currently held as rational among white people (Dixson and Rousseau, 2005). The use of stories in CRT literature helps to unpack racism in terms of how race privileges some while hegemonizing others (Dixson & Rousseau, 2005; Parker & Lynn, 2002). Solórzano and Yosso (2002) call for methods that utilize stories as a base to bring forward the ways in which racial privilege operates; thus, the use of counterstories may prove useful in helping white researchers examine our own racial narratives, stories, and identities which are often unexamined, and ultimately not simply tell stories for the sake of the story. Examining racial narratives makes visible the ways in which white people create and maintain racism and privilege. The interrogation of "life" narratives and experiences serves to disrupt what white people historically hold to be normative and raceless or color-blind (Bonilla-Silva, 2003).

Whiteness as Property
Harris (1995) outlines the conditions by which society constructs whiteness as property. The notion of whiteness as property implies that there is a certain ab-

soluteness or inalienability to whiteness. According to Harris (1995), although this absoluteness traditionally precludes something as having value as property, people vested in the value of whiteness experience a high sense of value. Paradoxically, Harris (1995) contends that whiteness is infinitely an absolute; one drop of white blood can never make one white, yet one drop of blood can strip one of whiteness, and thus decrease her or his value.

Often falsely understood at the level of phenotype (Hall, 1997; Montague, 1997; Winant, 2000), to possess whiteness is an absolute that garners a higher value as property. Harris (1995) cites that white people capitalize on their whiteness for purposes of enjoyment, placing high value on the reputation of whiteness. For example, calling white people *Black* can cause harm to their reputation and thus devalue one's whiteness. Conversely, calling Black people *white* causes those people no harm and gives the "absolute and inherent goodness" of being white. Finally, whiteness excludes insofar as white people never have to define what whiteness is, but rather are continually defining what it is not. In defining what whiteness is not, white people are able to exclude all of those who they deem to not possess whiteness. In conjunction, the nature of how whiteness is not defined, along with the absolute nature of whiteness, provides a space whereby whiteness serves a property function (Harris, 1995; Morrison, 1992).

Expansive and Restrictive Views of Anti-discrimination

In examining CRT as a theoretical framework, it is important to note that CRT scholars examine the distinctions between an expansive and a restrictive view of anti-discrimination and anti-discrimination law (Crenshaw, 1995; Dixson & Rousseau, 2005; Tate & Rousseau, 2002). Crenshaw (1995) believes that an expansive view of the law stresses equality as a result. In the expansive view, a broad net is cast with full recognition that racism, discrimination, and subjugation work in concert, not isolation. Thus, expansive views of anti-discrimination policies conceive of ending the conditions and circumstances by which the subordination of Black people exists and working with the courts and governmental agencies "to further the national goal for eradicating the effects of racial oppression" (Crenshaw, 1995, p. 105). Those arguing for expansive understandings recognize discriminatory acts and practices as systemic and not isolated individualized targets against people of color. Expansive views of race most align with a narrative where a white teacher, as in the case of this research project, moves beyond herself or himself, and begins to understand the complexities of race and her or his own implication as an overt and covert racist. Such a narrative would prompt a change in practice toward redressing racist, discriminatory, and subjugating pedagogical practices.

Conversely, restrictive legal views on anti-discrimination are oriented and focused on the process rather than the outcomes of the process (Crenshaw, 1995; Dixson & Rousseau, 2005; Tate & Rousseau, 2002). The restrictive view values a look toward the future, toward what anti-discrimination policies can do in potential cases and circumstances, making no effort to "redress present manifestations of past injustice" (Crenshaw, 1995, p. 105). Restrictionists pose that discriminatory acts take place in isolation, are targeted at individuals, and are not representative of a social policy against an entire group; such an orientation protects restrictionists from dealing with race outside very narrowly constructed, localized, and ahistorical experiences or contexts.

The restrictionist view consequently supports Bell's (1995b) notion of interest convergence. Interests in redressing discrimination are always set against the "competing interests of white people, even when those interests were actually created by the subordination of Black people" (Crenshaw, 1995, p. 105). Bell (1995b) states that the "interest of Black people in achieving racial equality will be accommodated only when it converges with the interests of white people" (p. 22), highlighting that white people who engage in restrictive notions of anti-discrimination also value laws that support restrictive ideals. Engaging with expansionist views oriented beyond process and toward actual outcomes is in conflict with white interests (Bell, 1995b).

Considering the narratives of white teachers is important and aligns with the restrictive view of CRT to examine the extent to which teachers espouse color-blind rhetoric or other stances that discredit the epidemic nature of racism. Such teachers' narratives might help to reveal when teachers do not take into account the historical implications of race or see how their racial trajectory, both in narrative and identity, is influenced by the problematic nature of race in the United States. Teachers expressing such restrictive narratives might believe that race is not significant and place the onus of learning directly on the student as opposed to looking at the student as part of a racialized, gendered, sexualized, (dis)abled group and think about the implications of her or his own narrative as shaping their pedagogical beliefs (Dixson & Fasching-Varner, 2008).

White Racial Identity Theory (WRIT)

Racial identity has been explored as a process of coming to know one's self as an individual (Erikson, 1963, 1968) coupled with "one's perception that he or she shares a common heritage with a particular racial group" (Helms, 1990, p. 3; as well as Cross, 1978; Cross, Paraham, & Helms, 1991). Racial identity accordingly represents "the subjective understanding of oneself as a racialized person [with] the recognition that one is both *similar to* and *different from* other people" (Rockquemore & Arend, 2003, p. 51). Across races, the concept and development of racial identity has looked significantly different. For many people of color, sense and understanding of identity have been predicated on the hegemony of white supremacy (West, 1990). For white people, white supremacy has created spaces for white racial identity to remain invisible and unnamed (Frankenberg, 1993).

The scholarship of Frankenberg (1993, 1996a, 1996b, 1997, 1999, 2001, 2005) and Helms (1984, 1990, 1992a, 1992b, 1993, 1994, 1995, 1997) is significant and contributory to the development of the study of white racial identity. As such, it is imperative to outline WRIT from the perspective of both Frankenberg and Helms in understanding WRIT as a theoretical tool.

Frankenberg (1993) concluded that whiteness is an ever-changing construct, a "product of local, regional, national and global relations" across time (p. 236). Frankenberg (2005) asserts that in order to understand the experience of being white, white people must work toward "transforming the meaning of whiteness and to transforming the relations of race in general" (p. 242). As such, Frankenberg (2005) suggests that to explore whiteness and white racial identity, white people must explore how whiteness serves as a marker to "the production and reproduction of dominance, subordination, and normativity, marginality, and privilege" (pp. 236–237). Furthermore, Frankenberg (2005) asserts that whiteness is a location of structural advantage, or race privilege. Second, it is a "standpoint," a place from which white people look at themselves, at others, and at society. Third, "whiteness" refers to a set of cultural practices that are usually unmarked and unnamed (Frankenberg, 2005). Throughout her work, Frankenberg (1993, 1996a, 1996b, 1997, 1999, 2003, 2005) revisits the notion that whiteness, as an operating hegemonic force, confers privilege along lines of race. Ironically, the greatest recipients of this privilege have refused to acknowledge whiteness both as a race and as a source of privilege. While Frankenberg does not directly explore white racial identity as such, Howard (2000) highlighted that Frankenberg's work is among the most used paradigms for thinking about white racial consciousness. Frankenberg's work contributes to white racial identity research in that the examination of white racial narratives provides a potential link to pedagogical practices to which educators ascribe.

While other models of white identity exist (see, for example, Gaetner, 1976; Ganter, 1977; Jones, 1972; Kovel, 1970; Terry, 1977), it is the work of Helms (1984, 1990, 1992a, 1992b, 1993, 1994, 1995, 1997, 2003) that has served a critical role in the discourse of white racial identity. Helms developed White Racial Identity Theory (WRIT) out of the Nigresence Racial Identity Development models of the 1970s and 1980s (Akbar, 1974; Banks, 1981; Cross 1971, 1978; Dizzard, 1971; Gay, 1984). Helms believed that a model of white racial identity theory must necessarily recognize that white people move through, between, and circularly through stages or statuses of development. Helms (1990) furthermore posited that the model must not be disconnected from a focus on the self and one's "unresolved racial development issues" (p. 53). Thus, Helms (1984, 1990, 1992a, 1992b, 2003) developed and refined a model of racial identity for white people that could productively engage them in coming to terms with their own identity.

Helms's model of white racial identity asserts that there are six racial identity statuses. A great deal of naïveté exists in the first stage, the contact status, as the person "does not consciously think of herself/himself as white" (Helms,

1992, p. 37). White people may know that racial groups exist in the contact stage, but they exert great effort to use color-blind discourse to "minimize differences in treatment due to race" (Helms, 1992, p. 38). In the contact status, a white person might articulate an "I am innocent" or "It's not my fault" approach. The white person in the contact status, moreover, may have limited experiences with people of color and may use these experiences to teach him/her about race or diversity.

In the disintegration status, white people move to a "How can I be white?" approach that revolves around "guilt and confusion" (Helms, 2003, p. 50). In this status, one might attempt to balance relationships with white people and Black people, often turning to white people to seek resolution of guilty feelings and learning that "when interacting with people of color, if he or she wants to be accepted by other White people, then he or she must violate moral and ethical principles" (Helms, 1992a, p. 46). At this point in the racial identity model, confusion often forces the white person to move back toward contact status or firmly internalize racist beliefs (Helms, 2003).

The third status, known as "reintegration", encompasses both covert and overt racist beliefs, with "hostility and anger directed toward people of color" (Helms, 1992, p. 53). Negative stereotypes, claims of reverse racism, and a total denial of racism generally characterize this status (Helms, 1984, 1990, 2003). White people in the reintegration status believe they are more successful than people of color because they are better and work harder than people of color. In this status, either a firm resistance to alternate models of thinking is established to reinforce white supremacist thought, or white people "gain a firmer conscious hold on their Whiteness" (Helms, 1992, p. 55). These first three statuses are part of what Helms (1984, 1990, 1992a, 2003) calls the abandonment of racism phase. The other three statuses move into a phase of evolution toward a non-racist identity.

The first status in the evolution of a non-racist identity is the pseudo-independence status; what had been once comfortable racist beliefs are no longer as comfortable (Helms, 2003). A white in this status begins "to acknowledge the responsibility of White people for racism and how he or she willingly and unwillingly perpetrates racism" (Helms, 1990, p. 61). White people in the pseudo-independence status are marked as race traitors and non-white people are suspicious of their intentions (Helms, 1990). The pseudo-independent white works toward "convincing other White people that racism has virtually vanished and defining for people of color how they should think, feel, and behave in order" to end racism (Helms, 1990, p. 61).

The fifth status is immersion/emersion, and the white person is searching "for a personally meaningful definition of whiteness and re-education of other White people about race and racism" (Helms, 2003, p. 52). Immersion/emersion requires that the white person "replace White and Black myths and stereotypes" and reflect on the meaning of history of both whiteness and Blackness in the context of the United States (Helms, 1990, p. 62). Immersion/emersion is thought to be difficult to engage with because it requires a white person to "assume personal responsibility for racism and to understand one's role in perpetuating it" (Helms, 1992, p. 74).

In the autonomy stage, the last status of the WRIT model, the white person reflects on "a lifelong process of discovery in which the person truly values diversity" (Helms, 1992a, p. 87). Crucial to autonomy is that white people discover self and others through authentic engagement by being "continually open to new information and new ways of thinking about racial and cultural variables" (Helms, 1990, p. 66). Helms (1990, 1992, 1993) believes that autonomy is a lifelong process and, as such, white people may move back and forth through other previous statuses as they continue working toward developing a healthy racial identity as characterized by the autonomy status.

The premise of Helms's work with WRIT is that white people benefit from and are privileged by race. Despite the benefits and privilege of whiteness, white people often enact a color-blind approach to understanding race so as to rebuff, warp, and suppress minds (Helms, 2003). Helms (2003) believes the white racial identity model could provide a means to help white people develop a "healthy racial identity" (p. 241). Helms's model also recognizes that white privilege, as explored in social sciences and the humanities, provides some complexity to examining white people's belief systems. In addition, WRIT scholarship illuminates the ways in which white people engage in color-blind discourses in their public narratives to mask their private beliefs about people of color.

To that extent, the research presented in this book, which is situated in the narratives of white pre-service teachers about their experiences, lives, and teaching beliefs, contributes to understanding how pedagogical practices are shaped by belief systems informed by racial identity. As a theoretical framework, WRIT helps to make transparent what might otherwise be the private narratives of race.

Significance of Studying White Racial Identity

It is important to know what is significant about studying white racial identity with pre-service teachers while reading this text. Studying the racial narratives of white teachers and their relevance to the particular pedagogical belief systems of the teachers is significant in at least three ways. First, children of color are not performing well in school, as measured by problematic assessments in a schooling system that is dominated by white people. The success of students of color from any historically underrepresented group is crucial as we navigate through the twenty-first century, given the changing nature of demographics and a desire for our society to continue being both literate and productive; all children need to have equitable access to the education requisite in being literate and productive.

Second, the demographic composition of the United States teaching force has remained largely stable with an overwhelming majority of white teachers. Over the last twenty years, the teaching force has been comprised of 85% to 92% white teachers, signaling that white teachers essentially control educational opportunities for all students. Teacher decisions about where to work, how to teach, and how to socialize children is not a theoretical discussion. The makeup of the teaching force and the relatively low number of teachers of color represent urgency as we think about how to provide successful experiences for all children. Fifty-three percent of white students are likely to have a K–12 school experience with less than 5% of their peers coming from historically underrepresented groups (Fry, 2007). This data suggests that white people, too, are learning important messages about what it means to be white. White educators teach white children as much about the experience of being white as they teach these messages to students of color. Thus, understanding the narratives of white preservice teachers and how these narratives translate into teaching practices is vital as we look to the types of socialization experiences children will have.

Finally, as reported by CNN (Associated Press, 2003), many white teachers are fleeing predominately Black schools. In the 1999–2000 school year, for example, 31% of white teachers quit their jobs where the student population was 70% or more Black. Those teachers who remained worked in schools with lower populations of Black and poor pupils. These statistics are unlikely to change without better understanding the force of teachers' identities in the teaching and socialization processes in schools. Captured in narratives, teacher belief systems can inform how to staff schools and also how to find educators who can commit to the success of children attending schools with historically under-represented students. Evans (2003), of the National Association for the Advancement of Colored People, reported that he was not surprised that "young white teachers leave for the suburbs after a year or two. Many teachers, especially young women, are scared of Black neighborhoods."

The research presented in this text is of particular interest to teacher education programs when considering how to work with teacher candidates to prepare them as teachers for the twenty-first century. Moreover, this text is intended to help teacher educators make sense of racial narratives, particularly be reworking the frameworks by which we understand White Racial Identity (WRI), and how the new structure for understanding WRI might be useful to disrupt whiteness. Children of color are likely to continue being taught by predominately white teachers, and thus a concerted effort needs to be made to help teachers break through socialization cycles to provide more culturally responsive, congruent, and effective pedagogies (Dixson, 2005; Dixson & Fasching-Varner, 2008; Ladson-Billings, 1995). Furthermore, white teachers can develop a better understanding of how to productively and meaningfully work with students who are different from them in productive and meaningful ways (Dixson & Fasching-Varner, 2008; Fasching-Varner, 2006, 2009).

To help structure your reading of this book, the text is organized into three parts. The first part includes the previous reading (chapter 1) and a chapter that looks at the relevant literature in WRI and CRT (chapter 2). A methodological chapter (chapter 3) maps the terrain of how the study of pre-service teachers' narratives was conducted for this particular study, and commentary about how others may pursue similar studies methodologically. The third part is the heart of the book and provides an examination of pre-service teachers' naïve rationales for entering the profession (chapter 4), the semantic moves used by study participants to talk about race (chapter 5), and, finally, a detailed exploration of white racial identity including an exploration of a new way to think about WRI within a non-developmental framework (chapter 6). The third section ends with concluding thoughts that include implications and recommendations based on the research and directions for future research (chapter 7).

Chapter 2
Racial Identity & Pre-service Teachers

Introduction

In the first chapter of this book, I presented my vision of a multi-layered set of challenges in twenty-first century education that centers on disconnects between teachers and students in racial identity. Additionally, I presented some articulation of what I see as the theoretical frameworks by which we might best understand the challenges I presented, particularly as they relate to White Racial Identity. In this chapter, I examine the extant theoretical and empirical scholarship relevant to the theoretical framework of racial identity; I also study the complexities of racial identity in education and, specifically, I examine literature on race and racial identity models, including a specific focus on models of white racial identity development. Additionally, I examine literature related to pre-service teachers with respect to race and identity since the major focus of the text is on pre-service teacher populations.

Racial Identity Models in Theoretical Literature

Since the early 1970s, a variety of theorists have proposed that the study of racial identity is salient to the understanding of "various groups of color" (Helms, 1994, p. 21). While the general study of race includes Asian, Latino/a, and Indigenous groups (see Sue & Sue, 1971, 1972; and Lowery, 1983, respectively), it has been Black groups that have received significant theoretical and empirical research relative to racial identity (Carter & Helms, 1988; Helms, 1994). From the 1970s through the early 1980s, a number of models were developed to explore Black racial identity, also referred to as "Nigrescence" (see Akbar, 1974; Banks, 1981; Dizzard, 1971; and Gay, 1984, as examples). According to Gay (1984), each of the models of Nigrescence Racial Identity Development (NRID) "accounts for an ideological metamorphosis" of identity, all of which ultimately move individuals from negative to positive conceptualizations of self (p.44). The Nigresence models of racial identity served as an important framework or base in the development of other racial identity models.

While various NRID's have served in the larger discourse on identity development, Cross' (1971, 1978) model of Nigrescence best sets the stage for Helms's eventual creation of a white identity model; Cross (1971) first proposed a model of racial identity. Nigrescence was positioned as a conversion from "Negro-to-Black" for Black liberation from white hegemony with the express goal of understanding how "Black people move from a stage of racial consciousness characterized by self-abasement and denial of their Blackness, to a stage characterized by self-esteem and acceptance of their Blackness" (Helms, 1984, p. 154). Specifically analyzing the awareness involved in converting from "Negro" to "Black" in racial identity, Cross (1978) developed a four-stage model "characterized by self-concept issues concerning race and parallel attitudes about Blacks and White people as reference groups" (Helms, 1990, p. 19).

Similarly, a number of white racial identity models began to formulate in the 1970s and 1980s (Kovel, 1970; Jones, 1972; Gaertner, 1976; Ganter, 1977; Terry, 1977; and ultimately Helms, 1984). Prior to the development of Helms's model of white racial identity, other models had "focused on defining racism" through the creation of categories or typologies with the "implicit assumption that racism was only damaging to the victims of the resulting oppression" (Helms, 1990, p. 50). The early theories had not aptly or consciously considered the effect of the racism "on the beneficiaries or perpetrators of racism" themselves (Helms, 1990, p. 50).

Helms's Early Critiques of Identity Models

A threefold critique of the early models of white identity development surfaced in the literature. First, Helms (1990), did not believe that the theorists of the time had properly speculated "about the harmful consequences of racism on the perpetuators of racism," given that they did not focus on the positive development of white racial identity (p. 50). Second, the extant models were limited by static categorizations, not recognizing that people probably move between stages (later renamed "statuses") depending on life experiences (Helms, 1990, 1992a, 1992b, 1993). Finally, Helms believed that a model of white racial identity could not be disconnected from a focus on the self and one's "unresolved racial development issues" if it was to move beyond using non-white people as the means for white people to understand their own racial issues (Helms, 2003). In other words, white people must acknowledge an "awareness of personal responsibility for racism" (Helms, 1990, p. 53). To address these concerns, Helms (1984, 1990, 1992a, 1992b, 2003) developed and refined a model of racial identity that could productively engage white people in coming to terms with their own identity. As previously discussed, the model moves through a variety of status, from so-called racial naïveté to a sort of racial nirvana.

Significance of White Privilege and Color-Blindness

Two significant premises of white racial identity models are that, first white people benefit from and are privileged by race, and second despite benefits and privileges, white people often enact color-blind approaches to understanding race. According to Helms (1990), color-blind approaches, along with white privilege, act "to deny, distort, and repress minds," and, as such, Helms believes that models of racial identity may help white people "to develop a healthy White racial identity" (p. 241).

White Privilege
White privilege has been explored by a variety of researchers including, but not limited to, Roediger (1991, 1994, 1997, 1998); Solomon, Portelli, Daniel, and Campbell (2005); Lipsitz (1998, 2005, 2006); and Rothenberg (2004), whose collection of essays on privilege include authors such as hooks, Tatum, and Roediger. Despite the number of authors who write on white privilege, it is McIntosh's (1989) examination of white racial privilege that continually surfaces as dominating the discourse. McIntosh (1989) presents a simplistic yet easy-to-understand vista for educators into white privilege, conceptualizing white privilege as a knapsack full of privileges in the shape of "tools, maps, guides, codebooks" (p. 1) which white people carry, even when they "may not be consciously aware" of the privileges possessed (Helms, 1993, p. 241). The privilege of whiteness in part explains Helms's (1993) concern that white people ignore the benefits gained from racism, and how benefits come at the expense of non-white racial groups. Feagin and Vera (1995) complement Helms's thoughts, conceptualizing that ignoring racism and refusing to take responsibility for the ways in which white people perpetuate racism is further demonstrative of the white privilege manipulated to the benefit of white people. An absence of researchers personally working through the privileges of whiteness has afforded what appears to be a hallmark feature of many of the studies on whiteness and white privilege; the works become treatises that focus on what is wrong without critical examination of the researchers' own level of complicit and implicit participation.

Color-Blind Approaches
The works of Bonilla-Silva (2003, 2006); Williams (1997); Leonard (2004); Thompson (2003); and Ferber (2003) succinctly address Helms's premise concerning color-blind approaches with which white people engage relative to race. In a color-blind approach, white people assume that the playing field between

people of color and non-people of color is equal and level (Bonilla-Silva, 2003; Williams, 1997). To demonstrate this stance, white people often evoke the civil rights movement, professional athletes of color, entertainers of color, politicians, and now a president of color, or cite a friend who is a person of color, to demonstrate equality amongst groups (Ferber, 2003; Leonard, 2004; Thompson, 2003, 2004). Thus, white people have a sense that success is based on merit, and this is central to the use of color-blind discourse. Always implicit is the assumption that white people possess merit and people who are not white do not possess merit. Consequently, the dominant group believes anyone whom they deem as not working hard enough or making bad choices should not rewarded. In color-blind thought, race is not believed to be the reason why inequities exist (Bonilla-Silva, 2003; Williams, 1997). Cited by Bonilla-Silva (2003) as being part of new racism, color-blind racism distinguishes itself in that it is liberal sounding in nature, thus markedly distinct from the racism of the past. Bonilla-Silva (2003) argues that

> contemporary racial inequality is reproduced through "New Racism" practices that are subtle, institutional, and apparently non-racial. In contrast to the Jim Crow era, where racial inequality was enforced through overt means (e.g., signs saying "No Niggers Welcomed Here" or shotgun diplomacy at the voting booth), today racial practices operate in "now you see it, now you don't" fashion. (p. 3)

Color-blind racism works in tandem with white privilege, (re)inscribing each other's presence and producing what Bonilla-Silva (2003) calls "racism lite," which allows white people to avoid "naming those who it subjects and those who it rewards" (p. 3). The subtle nature of color-blind racism highlights the need for racial identity models that will help white people to name their racism and to work toward dismantling its scaffolding.

White Racial Identity Perspectives

After the development of Helms's model, a number of researchers in the fields of counseling, anthropology, sociology, and broadly conceived education applied the WRI model and examinations of whiteness to their own research. This section of the literature review is intended to provide a brief snapshot of the work on white racial identity and whiteness that has situated itself within Frankenbergian and Helmsian traditions.

The presence of "Whiteness," and whiteness's connection to racial identity is evident when examining literature across disciplines by researchers such as Applebaum (2007); Carter, Helms, and Juby (2004); Giroux (1997); Hartigan (1999); Hurtado (1999); Ignatiev (1995, 1997a, 1997b), Lipsitz (1998, 2005, 2006); López (2006); Philipsen (2003); Reason (2007); Roediger (1991, 1994,

1997, 1998, 2004); and Smedley (1998). In this literature, a common theme is a commitment to examining whiteness in the context of continually changing cultural environments. Hurtado (1999) summarizes the nature of the exploration of whiteness in the late twentieth and early twenty-first centuries as necessary and important work given that "we have yet to chronicle how those who oppress make sense of their power in relationship to those they have injured" (p. 226).

By exploring whiteness from a variety of perspectives, as through the lenses "of literary and film critics, historians, sociologists, and anthropologists," theories of whiteness are thought to be exploring the "powerful means of critiquing the reproduction and maintenance of systems of racial inequality"—whether or not such critique has been met is squarely up for debate (Hartigan, 1999, p. 183). Similarly, Lipsitz (2005, 2006) affirms the necessity for the critical study of whiteness to ensure that white people do not "portray the victims of racism as the beneficiaries of unearned privileges ignoring the possessive investment in whiteness and invert the history of racial politics in the United States" (2005, p. 112).

Reason (2007) and Watts (2007) believe that critical examination of whiteness cannot be achieved without white people's being able to articulate what whiteness means. Watts (2007) in particular believes that both the personal and political aspects of whiteness can be better understood once critical consciousness is developed, and Reason (2007) suggests critical consciousness does not develop when white people maintain their already-possessed articulations of whiteness. Reason (2007) in part suggests that many contemporary white people accept race as a social construction yet use the nature of the social construction to dismiss the reality of race. The literature suggests that researchers must understand that "accepting race as a social and political construction must not imply that race does not exist" or, worse yet, that race does not matter (p. 128). For Reason (2007), helping white people articulate their understandings, examining their narratives, and then re-articulating their understandings after learning experiences, is a method to help white people move beyond typical articulations of whiteness' meaning. Conversely, Giroux (1997) attempts to locate the conversation on whiteness within historic frames as a means of helping white people to develop agency with respect to their whiteness. Giroux (1997) claims that "the politics of racial privilege is fraught with fear and anger that accompany having to rethink one's identity," suggesting that when we "address the histories that shaped the normative space, practices and diverse relationships," we may be better able to temper white people's fears of dealing with the nature of race (p. 313). Like Giroux, Philipsen (2003) believes it is necessary to examine race, and whiteness in particular, with a focus on the historical nature of racial identity. Without situating the conversation on whiteness and race in historic terms, Philipsen (2003) believes that what is achieved is akin to "a disparate hodge-podge of things, one that is used routinely as a substitute for culture, place of origin, ethnicity, common traditions, and class, or as a convenient outlet for any number of prejudices and fears" (p. 199).

In a comprehensive examination of racial and ethnic identity, McDermott and Samson (2005) highlight that an "identification of whiteness with social responsibility is a frequent theme in current work on white racial identity" and whiteness (p. 249). Applebaum (2007) also explored the nature of social responsibility for whiteness in her study of white culpability and liability with respect to race and racism. Applebaum (2007) attempted to make sense of what it means when white people believe that they do not recognize or attach meaning to race, thus dismissing the importance of race. Applebaum (2007) suggests that "before social justice educators can contemplate what to do to promote student engagement, they must consider what is supporting student disengagement" (p. 465). Once student racial disengagement is understood, white students' discomfort can be addressed through the nature of their discomfort. Unfortunately, the literature that examines social responsibility for whiteness often approaches the work from the idea that students need to feel comfortable in order to better deal with the social, political, and moral responsibilities white people have to race. The prospective of providing comfort appears rather limiting as it does the very thing Applebaum (2007) claims her work does not do; by addressing white students' level of comfort with the topic of race, her work does not re-center white emotions as being that which matters (p. 467).

Edited Volumes on White Racial Identity and Whiteness

In addition to individual pieces of scholarly texts, a number of edited volumes on whiteness and critical studies of whiteness began being published in the mid-1990s. Current and significant volumes include Delgado and Stefancic's (1997) *Critical White Studies*; Hill's (1997) *Whiteness: A Critical Reader*; Brown et al.'s (2003) *Whitewashing Race*; Clark and O'Donnell's (1999) *Becoming and Unbecoming White*; Hitchcock's (2002) *Lifting the White Veil*; Frankenberg's (1997) *Displacing Whiteness*; and Newman's (2007) *Identities & Inequalities*. Each of these collections dedicates its focus to critical examinations of whiteness, making whiteness and its associated privileges and racist orientations visible and transparent to readers through a combination of theoretical, empirical, autobiographical, and auto-ethnographic contributions.

Most volumes on whiteness and white identity examine the concept of whiteness in particularly neutral and/or disconnected ways from the volumes' authors. Volumes on whiteness and white identity emphasize the problems with whiteness and use examples and ideas to help white people understand the historical meaning of whiteness while also attempting to have white people work against the privilege that whiteness confers. The works, however, never situate the authors within their own experiences. There are disconnected critical examinations of whiteness such as Hill's (1997) *Whiteness: A Critical Reader*, a twenty-one-chapter, edited volume on whiteness that draws from twenty-four contemporary authors, many of whom are considered well respected scholars such as Roediger, Giroux, and Ignatiev. While whiteness in Hill's volume is presented from many perspectives which outline and critique the nature of whiteness, the orientation is ultimately achieved by looking at whiteness in abstract situations removed from the authors' personal experiences. These edited volumes socialize readers to a mechanism whereby whiteness can be talked about yet simultaneously can be distanced from personal responsibility for one's whiteness.

Each of the volumes differs in its examination and focus of significant areas of whiteness. Frankenberg (1997) cautions readers of edited volumes on whiteness to understand that such volumes "trace the intermeshing of whiteness with other webs of relations," and, as such, readers can get lost on understanding whiteness from so many disparate perspectives (p. 21). Frankenberg also suggests that readers understand that "analyzing whiteness is inseparable from the critique of racism," and therefore whiteness' link to racism and racist orientations should not be far from the reader's mind, despite the directions the volumes on identity take (p. 21).

Works such as Clark and O'Donnell's (1999) *Becoming and Unbecoming White* can be linked to the ideas of Frankenberg and help give shape to the necessity of the work that examines the natures of whiteness and racism, asserting that "racism cannot simply be removed from the cultural, social, and political arenas by calling for its abolition or be appealing to calls for justice" (p. 3). Clark and O'Donnell present a variety of chapters edited by leading scholars in the field and examine both whiteness and whiteness relative to the conversation on racism. Of all the edited volumes on whiteness and white racial identity, the Clark and O'Donnell (1999) text purposefully solicited chapters in which white authors told and examined their stories against the theoretical literature and focused on how whiteness and white racism operate both at individual and societal levels.

Racial Identity and Counseling

The works of Sue (1992, 1993); Sue and Sue (1971, 1972, 1990); Ponterotto (1989); and Reynolds and Baluch (2001) have been significant in examining the relationship between racial identity and counseling. Ponterotto (1989) argues that racial identity is important for incorporation into counseling research as it seeks to help counselors understand what it is that a particular person brings to her or his experience through whiteness; additionally, the counselor's own racial identity brings different meanings to the counseling interaction. The works of Sue (1992, 1993) and Sue and Sue (1971, 1972, 1999) are particularly invested in understanding racial identity for counselors when there appears to be a disconnect between the counselor and client. Sue (1992) and Sue and Sue (1990) hope that racial understanding between counselor to client and back to counselor can be the foreground where trusting relationships are built. Sue (1993) has expressed particular concern, impatience, and anger at the often slow process of relationship building and trust relative to race. Sue (1992), and Sue and Sue (1990) hope that racial understanding, from counselor and client and back to counselor, can be the foreground upon which trusting relationships are built.

Reynolds and Baluch (2001) are vocal critics of the current approach and understanding of racial identity counseling research, outlining that conversation on race has traditionally been limited in focus to white and Black racial identity. Sue and Sue (1999) challenge counseling researchers to extend beyond Black and white counseling models of racial identity to include Asian, Indigenous, and Latino/a groups and to more robustly address concerns of trust and relationship building in the work of counselors.

Racial Identity and Education

Researchers Asher (2007); Carter and Goodwin (1994); Chubbuck (2004); Cochran-Smith (2000); Hallman (2007); Hernandez Sheets (2001); Johnson (2002); Sleeter (2005); and Tatum (1994) have undergone significant theoretical explorations of racial identity and education. Sleeter (2005) theorizes that racial identity and "race matters because teachers bring to the classroom interpretations of students and their communities," and these understandings that teachers bring must be mediated by the teacher's very own racialized experiences (p. 243). Sleeter's (2005) sentiments are echoed and extended by Johnson (2002), who cites that the high percentage of white teachers in the United States, most of whom are "increasingly teaching children racial, cultural, and class backgrounds different from their own," necessitates the need for teachers to understand the nature of the mediated interpretations their race brings to the table (p. 153).

Asher (2007) broadens the conversation to include a variety of social intersections of difference, but ultimately recognizes that white people need to be "implicated in extant relations of power that reinforce the mythic norm" that serves as a national orientation as "the central point of reference for and definition of all others" (p. 65). Hernandez Sheets (2001) argues for the importance of whiteness in education and the necessity for examining the whiteness, yet is skeptical of the current approach; he believes that the current conversation too often locates conversations about whiteness, racism, and identity to single so-called diversity or multiculturalism courses where all issues of difference must be taught. Hallman (2007) attempts to explore teacher identity in a reductionist approach of teacher e-portfolios, claiming that the portfolio created in a single course would lead to transformative experiences with one's racial identity. Asher (2007) and Hernandez Sheets (2001) recognize the limited nature of such approaches to whiteness in education.

In her discussion of white allies and racism, Tatum (1994) further contributes to the critique of one-time approaches to teaching white students. Tatum

(1994) notes that such approaches reify vague understandings of race and encourage students to cite only typical or cliché examples of racist and non-racist white people, such as "past and present Klan leaders and conservative southern politicians" in the racist camp, and someone like "Viola Liuzzo" in the nonracist camp (p. 462). Tatum (1994), Asher (2007), and Hernandez Sheets (2001) all believe in the importance of getting white people to see themselves as implicated in the conversation, not reducing the conversation on whiteness solely to national figures of race.

Carter and Goodwin (1994) explore racial identity from both historic locations and from the perspectives of schoolchildren examining the "racial identity theory and research with examination of educational literature using racial identity theory as a conceptual lens" (p. 292); their exploration provides a significant focus on the racial identity school experiences of children of color. Carter and Goodwin (1994), however, assert that researching theories of racial identity are also significant from the perspectives of teachers since "the educational treatment of children of color has typically been (a) framed by the basic principles of the inferiority and deprivation paradigms and (b) often implemented by individuals characterized by low levels of racial identity" (p. 315).

Empirical Studies of White Racial Identity in Education

Regarding empirical studies in education, the literature suggests there is a limited body of studies that directly address white racial identity. Sleeter's (2001) description of the nature of professional development offered to teachers emphasizes the teachers' constructions of race vis-à-vis the students. Catalogna, Greene, and Zirkel's (1981) study examines race and racial identity and, like Sleeter's (2001) study, the focus of the research is on the teachers' perceptions of student race. McAllister and Irvine (2000) examine white racial identity models relative to teacher behavior by analyzing studies of teachers in schools. Studies conducted by Williams and Evans-Winter (2005) and Vargas (1999) discuss white racial identity; however, the focus of both studies is on how faculty of color educate white adult students. The common thread among this body of literature is the relative decontextualization of issues of race, moving away from the teachers themselves and focusing the conversation back to racialized others. Chubbuck (2004), however, examines whiteness differently, using a life history approach, working with two teachers' stories, suggesting that white racial identity is important because with the "external presence" of the research process it is often unlikely that dialogue on one's whiteness and white identity would occur without an intentional use of life history (p. 330).

A number of pseudo-empirical studies of race and whiteness are reductionist in nature and place over-focused emphasis on whiteness through pedagogical and methods-based approaches. Copenhaver-Johnson (2006) discusses an experience where she realized her daughter's classroom library lacked texts that presented perspectives from a variety of races. Instead of critically examining the nature of whiteness and how whiteness, as a form of white supremacist thinking, reifies the reasons why a classroom library would be so vacant of racial perspective, Copenhaver-Johnson redirects the focus of the conversation from adults to the children; she suggests that the reading of diversity books and "modify[ing] the expectations and participant structures of read aloud" are avenues to addressing issues of race (p. 18). In a similar methods-based approach, McDermott (2002) suggests that teachers' white racial identity could be addressed though the creation of collages with pre-service teachers, suggesting that "aesthetic representations of self problematize discourses" (p. 65). Further, McDermott argues that the collaging is helpful, given her suggestion for "a move in educational practice away from epistemologies, away from 'what' and toward 'when' and 'how'" (p. 358). Current scholarship and discourse place a significant emphasis in the discussion of teachers' white identity as being a conversation about methods. Such methods-based approaches miss the opportunity to understand the operating systems of the paradigm(s) in place that is the nature of racial truths, or ontologies, and the ways our systems of knowing, or epistemologies, become a vehicle for understanding ourselves as raced.

To highlight this "methods-based" approach, Brooks, Browne, and Hampton (2008), for example, steer considerations of race and teacher whiteness away from teachers and back to a reader-response pedagogical approach in working with novels and texts from authors as Sharon Flake. Brooks et. al (2008) suggest that the power of the work is how it serves in "deliberately disrupting gender and race-based social inequities through literature" (p. 667). By focusing on pedagogy and the practice of teacher, the teacher, her or his racial identity, and the implication of teacher whiteness are lost.

Parsons (2001) provides perhaps the most connected study of education that directly links to models of white racial identity. Parsons' (2001) work is with white male fourth graders and their use of racialized and gendered privilege. Although the teachers were also white, the focus is on children and so even in this work, the teachers' white racial identity is lost. Overall, the literature that examines white racial identity and education is not particularly robust, as most studies of whiteness have been situated in discourses beyond education and schooling. When the focus is in the realm of schooling and education, too often the emphasis is on a teaching methods approach; thus, teacher racial identity is lost.

Literature on Pre-service Teachers

Research has historically skirted the exploration of white racial identity of pre-service teachers. A search for extant literature revealed no identifiable studies that examined pre-service teachers' racial identity per se, and no exploration of how such an identity becomes operationalized in the daily experiences of "being" a teacher. Thus, I present the studies that most closely approach the topic and loosely structure them into three groups: (1) "historic" studies looking at race and prospective or in-service teachers (Brearley, 1947; Caliver, 1936; Catalogna, Greene, & Zirkel, 1981; Stephenson, 1952); (2) examination of initiatives and studies with pre-service teachers (Adams, Bondy, & Kuhel 2005; Cross, 1978; Cross, DeVaney, & Jones, 2001; Merseth, Sommer, & Dickstein, 2008; Lawrence & Tatum, 1997; Lee & Dallman, 2008; McIntyre, 2002; Tettegah, 1996; Wiggins, Follo, & Eberly, 2007; Wong, 2008); and (3) "general" theoretical pieces that look at instructors' experiences addressing difference with pre-service teachers (Gay & Kirkland, 2003; Gordon, 2005; Levine-Rasky, 1998; Marx & Pennington, 2003). Montecinos and Nielson's (2004) study did not fit within the categories provided above and will be discussed separately.

Historic Studies

In terms of historic studies, Caliver (1936) wrote in *The Journal of Negro Education* about the roles of teachers and teacher education in "the reorganization of education of Negroes" (p. 508), suggesting that teachers take an introspective examination of their own "complacency and vested interests" (p. 514). Caliver (1936) ultimately looked beyond white teachers, articulating his concern that Black students educated by primarily white teachers were subject to a form of intellectual slavery that would be worse than the physical slavery of the past. Caliver (1936) offered that white teachers were certainly welcome to help but that the solutions will not be found in "a Lincoln, nor a New England missionary, but it will be [found with] Negro teachers themselves" (p. 516). Brearley (1947) offers a theoretical position that prospective educators would benefit from thorough examination of themselves and their knowledge, in addition to "the cultural resources of the community" (p. 75). The culturally responsive offering made by Brearley suggests that if teachers undertake the task of teaching, they must also challenge what they "know" to be true if they hope to break from a euro/ethnocentric lens. Brearley (1947) offers that "ethnocentrism is based more upon tradition than upon experience; the skillful teacher may often effect a change by presenting a different interpretation of a familiar situation," namely, her or his racialized way of operating in the world (p. 76).

Although Catalogna, Greene, and Zirkel (1981) conducted research with teachers, the focus of this research was on the teachers' perceptions of students' race, not on the teachers' racial identity itself. While this research revealed interesting findings of what teachers conceptualize as being races, essentially a false association between ethnicity and race, it neither examined how teachers were socialized to their beliefs in racial categorization, nor did the study explore the teachers' sense of racial identity.

Stephenson's (1952) study most closely approached pre-service teachers as a population of research participants. Like Catalogna, Greene, and Zirkel (1981), Stephenson (1952) focused on teachers' perceptions of students to determine racial identity; however, the study did not focus on the teachers' exploration of racial identity relative to their own lives.

Studies with Pre-service Teachers and Initiatives

Various studies examine particular initiatives and studies of pre-service teachers relative to said pre-service teachers' whiteness. Merseth, Sommer, and Dickstein (2008) examine pre-service teacher identity narratives with Ivy League students who want to teach in urban areas; they suggest that investigating identities is important to how a pre-service teacher can think about teaching in diverse settings. Merseth, Sommer, and Dickstein fail to address the ways in which the white racial identity of the participants actually comes to bear, but rather focus more on how white teachers will approach teaching racial others. Wong (2008), on the other hand, suggests that studying pre-service teachers' experiences in multicultural courses necessitates the need for field components "providing the pre-service teachers with a culturally diverse experience" (p. 32). Like Merseth, Sommer, and Dickstein (2008), Wong (2008) discusses pre-service teacher identity in conceptualizing the project, but the work is a reduction away from examining pre-service teachers' whiteness and toward using methods and experiences to help said teachers learn how to work with so-called racial others.

Lee and Dallman (2008) and Adams, Bondy, and Kuhel (2005) discuss how white teachers can work with students who are "racial others" relative to the teacher's racial identity. Lee and Dallman (2008) explain that they believe "understanding is the most important thing in diversity" (p. 36), yet they use understanding with pre-service teachers to look at how to work with students when there is a race mismatch, rather than looking at the teachers' lives and whiteness. Lee and Dallman (2008) suggest that white pre-service teachers need to be better at "appreciating each child's similarities and differences" (p. 38). Adams, Bondy, and Kuhel (2005) similarly examine identity through the frame of helping white pre-service teachers learn what to do in "an unfamiliar setting" (p. 41). The pre-service teachers' growth with their whiteness was linked to how positive their experience was with students who were not white. While not critiquing the need for looking at similarities and differences, the focus is always placed on students and not on the white pre-service teachers about whom the work is based, and appears to limit the power of this work to move the field forward.

Attitudes on Racial Identity

Several studies examine attitudes about race and racial identity with mix-gendered participants. Tettegah (1996) examined attitudes of pre-service teachers relative to their white racial consciousness. As in the more historic research, Tettegah (1996) embedded research questions concerning pre-service teachers' perceptions about teaching students from racial groups different than their own.

While Tettegah (1996) attempted to address the teachers' racial identities, the results were gathered through survey data that focused on "others" rather than the teachers' thinking about their own racial identity. Wiggins, Follo, and Eberly (2007) suggested that giving white pre-service teachers immersion experiences in communities of color for field placement would help to improve "the attitudes of these pre-service teachers" relative to race (p. 653). Like Tettegah (1996), Wiggins, Follo, and Eberly (2007) relied on survey data collected from pre-service teachers in order to analyze the pre-service teachers' white racial identity. What is striking in both research studies is the necessity of using racial "others" to explore white racial identity, supporting Morrison's (1992) thesis that whiteness always exists only with the existence of a "darker" other.

Cross, DeVaney, and Jones (2001) explored the attitudes of pre-service teachers as those attitudes related to various spoken dialects. Like Tettegah (1996) and Wiggins, Follo, and Eberly (2007), Cross, DeVaney, and Jones (2001) used quantitative survey research to understand how a group of pre-service teachers judged dialects of five different speakers. This study sample was mixed gender and mixed race, ultimately producing findings that demonstrated that the white participants favored white speakers over Black speakers. Again, this research did not explore pre-service teachers' sense of racial identity, and used a variety of speakers across races to ascertain findings for the research.

Teacher Educator Reflections on Practice
A final series of studies focuses on teacher educators making sense of working with predominately white pre-service teachers. Gay and Kirkland (2003) study is a theory-rich piece that explored the necessity for pre-service teachers to develop "cultural critical consciousness" (p. 181). Gay and Kirkland (2003) concluded that white pre-service teachers benefit in terms of examining white racial identity when they are forced to move beyond conversation and to "actually engaging [in] real life experiences" rather than use conversations to escape from "the intellectual, emotional, psychological, moral, and pedagogical challenges inherent" in the work of being a teacher (p. 186). Similarly, Levine-Rasky (1998) called on teacher education programs to stop waiting for faculty of color to magically appear to do the work of addressing pre-service teachers' sense of white racial identity and understandings of multiculturalism, and stated that all faculty bear responsibility in engaging "issues of equity and difference in a way that helps teacher candidates understand their [un]consciousness and motivations" relative to race and pre-service teachers' white identity (p. 108).

Gordon (2005) relied not on theory, but rather on autobiography to examine her own particular experiences as a white female teacher educator working with pre-service teachers. Gordon (2005) did not situate her work within the larger scholarly discussion on racial identity, a critical gap, since her desire was that her research aid in understanding how race is operationalized in pre-service teacher education. Marx and Pennington (2003) crafted work similarly to Gordon (2005); they positioned their work, however, in the larger discussion of race, examining separate studies that they each conducted while working with white pre-service teachers. Problematic in the Marx and Pennington research is that the narrative engages in a self-congratulatory discourse for being "brave enough to undertake this kind of controversial work" (p. 107), referencing the examination of whiteness and white racial identity. The bravery discourse reveals a limit in problematizing the historic benefits and privileges associated with racism. For people of color, living with race has never been a conversation of being brave enough; people of color live with race whether or not they want to have to engage with race.

A final concern of Marx and Pennington's work is the conceptualization that Black children are "our children of color." Such a framing demonstrates a white liberal perspective that is consistent with Harris's conceptualization of the property value of whiteness and a liberal savior attitude. Marx and Pennington remove the focus from the pre-service teachers' critical understanding of their own race as a means to transmogrify the way in which they engage pedagogy, placing the focus on becoming the champions and saviors of Black children.

Finally, Montecinos and Nielsen (2004) presented a study unlike all the previous studies in its potential to address issues of racial identity for pre-service teachers. Despite a participant set of forty white male teachers, Montecinos and Nielson (2004) explored only issues of gender in their research. While they positioned that race and class are important, the lens for analysis of the participants' narratives was focused solely on gender.

Given the exploration of the extant literature that addresses pre-service educators, it becomes clear that currently there are no studies that directly examine white pre-service teachers' racial identities as such. Consequently, there are no resulting studies that examine white racial identity as candidates reach the end of their pre-service teacher education program and their ensuing transition from pre-service education program into their first teaching job.

Gaps in the Literature

Three gaps in education racial identity literature appears which could be addressed through qualitative-oriented research such as the research explored in this book. First, much of the extant literature speaks to the experiences and white racial identity of white educators by placing focus on how they come to know racialized others. While learning how to effectively work with students is in fact part of the mission of educators, there appears to be a lack of literature that examines how white pre-service teachers and white teacher educator researchers come to terms with their own whiteness. This gap leads to the second gap in the literature: there also appear to be no studies that examine the transition of teachers from pre- to in-service and these teachers' sense and understanding of white racial identity. As pre-service teachers leave their programs, questions arise: How prepared are they to deal with themselves? How prepared are white people to look at the ways in which their whiteness replicates white supremacy with negative effects for students? How well do pre-service teachers even understand why they are becoming teachers? What are the connections or lack of connections between their rationales for employment in education and their understanding of selves as white people?

The third and final gap points to the lack of voice in the literature as to how white racial identity models can be used as a means of analyzing and explicating the nature of individual white people, both white individuals and individuals who are part of the larger group of white people connected through whiteness.

Chapter 3
Mapping the Terrain

"CIRCUS, n. A place where horses, ponies, and elephants are permitted to see men, women, and children acting the fool."
Ambrose Bierce

The concept of circus is an interesting, albeit limited, metaphor–approach for what has been the vexing, privileged nature of research in education, and particularly research that looks to examine race and racial identity. Little (1993) argues that the circus has served the supposed purpose of creating a space "separated from the real world outside the tent by its appeal as a dazzling, monumental, and aggrandizing overflow of erotic and exotic representations of otherness" (p. 119). While not the explicit or named goal of qualitative research in education, our field has often situated itself within the same tradition in which Little (1993) situates the circus; the research circus is a place where groups of spectators, or educators, comes to watch the ringleader, the teachers, educators, and researchers, manage the spectacle of the clowns, animals, and performers, loosely conceptualized as the over-researched and underrepresented children of color in the United States, in a carefully rehearsed spectacle (Little, 1993). Education has always relied on an "other" to perform. Inherent to how the circus audience enacts its gaze, Little (1993) asserts that the audience, and perhaps the ringmaster, view and understand "the self as a stable, coherent, and bounded entity" (p. 120).

Generally in my work, and in the research for this book, I seek to shift or invert the focus of the gaze from "others" in qualitative educational research to the gazers, ourselves. Little (1993) highlights that the more intent the focus is on the viewing the other, "the more spastic, contradictory, and humiliating [the spectators'] actions become" in maintaining their othering gaze (p. 120). Little's understanding that the fools of the circus are really the spectators and not the animals or performers captures the delicious irony of qualitative educational research on race. White researchers have been spastic in a commitment to focusing the gaze on others, ignoring our own racial naïveté and arrogance, in an attempt to maintain, reify, and benefit from the white supremacist agenda created with the very first white invaders of the United States.

In this methodology, I hope to illuminate the path of my research by first briefly exploring my own researcher positionality, as well as some basic epistemological considerations inherent to my work. I will discuss the specific approaches and methods that were undertaken in conducting the research and then will discuss three considerations that were central in my thinking throughout the research process. Finally, I will end with the presentation of profiles of the participants in this study as a means of introducing the people whose words form a major part of this text.

Researcher Positionality

As a white male academic, I have struggled to understand and make sense of myself both in terms of how I am raced and gendered as well as how I reify gender and race supremacy with my whiteness as a primary hegemonizing force. Throughout my academic life, my own conceptualization of my research agenda has shifted significantly. This shift has come through my growing understandings of race and white racial identity, as well as understanding my role as a racist white male supremacist operating within a racist white supremacist male-dominated field of study in a racist white supremacist male-dominated institution, situated in a racist white supremacist male-dominated nation, in a racist white supremacist male-dominated global landscape. In this landscape being a white male has afforded white academics front-row seats at the research circus (hooks, 2003; Little, 1993).

Through a combination of teaching, academic, and personal experiences, I have come to understand the problematics of (my) whiteness (Fasching-Varner, 2009) and, more importantly, my express role as a hegemonizer in the larger and broader social landscape. When I started my doctoral program, for example, I was convinced that my intent to conduct research with predominately white research participants in Germany, framed by Goldhagen as ordinary people, could make a difference in education by showing that individual white Germans, now in their seventies, were not as problematic, as anti-Semitic, or as racist as they had been framed but rather were innocent bystanders of war and a more systemic operationalization of race. My initial research agenda as a young scholar derived from a necessity to protect the unnamed, perhaps unconscious, racial contract that had/has afforded me so many life privileges, and a malignant denial surrounding race that I share with the participants in this study (Mills, 1997). My experiences have reinforced that, particularly as an educator, I have a responsibility to know better and to do better, be it with respect to the research I conduct, the role I choose to take as an educator, or the type of person I choose to be. With time to grow first as a doctoral student and now as a scholar and faculty member, I have come to abandon the racist research agenda of which I was quite proud at one time.

According to Leonardo (2002), white people must begin "by naming white-ness and recognizing it as fundamental to their development" (p. 45). In order to name whiteness in my work with pre-service teachers generally, and in this study particularly, I use(d) methods that include oral history interviewing, semi-structured interviews, and some document analysis. Such methods help to build snapshots of participants and of the researcher and are situated in the actual language provided by the research constituents. The use of language that develops as a result of race research helps to warrant and instantiate assertions made through the use of actual participants' voices, as opposed to (dis)aggregated statistical information that may or may not help to get at the actual undergirding of the systems of knowing in place.

Researchers must be present not just to "harvest" data from participants but to also make ourselves the object of study, examination, and interrogation to best capitalize on our own positionality and privilege as a white researcher examining race. Helms (1993) offers that

> if the researcher is unable to examine the effects of her or his own racial development on her or his research activities, then the researcher risks contributing to the existing body of racially oppressive literature rather than offering illuminating scholarship. (p. 242)

The implication in Helms's words is that the researcher is not void of her or his own racial identity development, and that not only is the study of her or his own racial identity and experiences important, but the researcher becomes an epistemological analytical tool herself or himself. Given these positions, it is paramount to note that, in my work, I attempt to move beyond declaring what I believe to be my researcher subjectivity and positionality to actually place myself inside the focus of the study (Peshkin, 1988).

Epistemological Approach

How we researchers enter the paradigms that guide our work is an important consideration when conducting any research, especially research that hopes to examine race. We must enter our research within the realm of our epistemological capability and then align our research methodology with our systems of knowing (Toulmin & Leary, 1985). What does such an epistemological, methodological, paradigmatic approach to qualitative research look like?

In linking considerations of epistemology to method, I begin with the premise that "language is by far the most powerful and versatile medium of communication" (Gumperz, 1972, p. 43). Therefore, to understand race, I chose to engage with methods that illuminate the ways in which language, what is said and not said as well as what is written and not written, is our most powerful epistemological tool in gathering data and consequently in forming any analysis.

Denzin and Lincoln (2003b) caution researchers to enact research with "an attitude of engagement with a world that is ontologically absurd but always meaningful to those who live in it" (p. 139). To me, the limit of research engagement
continues to be a disparity between researchers' over-emphasized reliance on
methods to make sense of truth and the absence of an overall guiding paradigm.
The absurdity rests not with the nature of the truths of people—single truths
cannot be captured—but rather the absence of epistemological alignment to the
subjective, partial, and situated truths we believe to exist. The "absurd" and often profane use of method, rather than epistemology, to explore the nature of
truth, ignores and disenfranchises the very peoples the researcher typically casts
as ontologically absurd and "other." Denzin and Lincoln's (2003b) recognition
that the life and the truth of the life are meaningful to those who live it call for a
greater paradigmatic responsibility in the construction of research agendas. With
this concept in mind, I engaged three guiding principles in my work while studying pre-service teachers, principles served as a metric to ensure that my work
addresses problems that I am epistemologically capable of addressing. The three
guiding principles are:

   (1) A recognition that carefully orchestrated methods do not, in and of
       themselves, obtain ontologically rich understandings or "true results"
       (Lather, 1986, p. 259).

   (2) Epistemology, not ontology or method, provided the best entrance to
       the framing of the paradigm, given that the choice of method and path
       to "truths" is highly dependent on the positioning of systems of know-
       ing.

   (3) My status as a privileged white male necessitated a research agenda
       that cast a critical "othering" gaze on myself and other privileged
       whites and acknowledged that my epistemologies as a researcher have
       the propensity for being white supremacist in nature and come from a
       history of white supremacy.

These guiding principles serve as the epistemological foundation of my work
with pre-service teachers and have allowed me to address Geertz's (1977) offering that "man is an animal suspended in the webs of significance he himself has
spun" (p. 5). Enacting upon these three paradigmatic guidelines frames the act of
disentangling the cobwebs within the scope of the research I conduct with pre-
service teachers. I am reminded by Fine (1997) that research has involved "acts
of cumulative privileging quietly loaded up on whites," and consequently the
disentanglement of the privilege and significance we spin upon ourselves must
be an open and transparent process involving a commitment to change now and
over time (p. 57).

While my positionality and/or the epistemological considerations of the research methodology could themselves be the subjects of a study, I now move to outlining the research conducted for this study.

Research Design

The particular study that drives this book began with ten participants, each of whom completed the first phase of the research; nine participants completed the series of interviews for the study. All the names for participants, institutions, and locations are pseudonyms to protect the identity of the research participants and to keep the overall focus of this text on the challenges teacher educators are facing generally in terms of preparing mostly white females to teach diverse groups of students. Consequently, as you think about the participants throughout the remainder of the book, I urge you to think of their narratives and my analysis in terms of how this information might help us, as a field, move forward as opposed to judging the "goodness" or "badness" of the participants.

The participants for my study were drawn from a bachelor of education pre-service teacher education program at Righteous College in the Northeast of the United States. Righteous College has approximately four thousand undergraduate and graduate students and is located in a socioeconomically privileged suburb near the medium-sized urban area of Lilac. The teacher education program at Righteous College prepares pre-service educators to work with students in grades one through twelve with specializations in childhood, adolescent, and special education.

Participants for this study represented what Patton (1990) has called a "purposive sample." Specifically, choosing participants from this teacher education program allowed for both a criterion and homogenous sample (Patton, 1990). The criteria for this homogenous group were that the participants were white and candidates in the teacher preparation program. The sample of participants was convenient to the extent that the program's white pre-service educators were completing their teacher education program and transitioning toward becoming in-service teachers. Righteous College was an institution of higher education with which I was familiar in my work as an educator in the Northeast. Also, the program articulated a commitment and purported explicit focus on diversity and equity; candidates were required to take a course in which they explored issues and concepts related to equity and diversity in education, a further criteria of interest for this study.

E-mails were sent to candidates in the program explaining the nature of the proposed research study and soliciting volunteers for the study. Fifteen teacher candidates responded and were provided with more information about the project and potential interview times. Five females and five males agreed to participate in the research study initially; one male participant did not finish the study.

I juxtaposed my own experiences within and against the narratives of the pre-
service teachers in my analysis and, to that extant, I am an auto-ethnographic
participant in the study.

Data Collection Methods

Concerned that the research methods aligned with my systems of knowing, I
engaged participants in a series of two interviews using the particular concept of
testimony to address the "importance of those who are historically invisible having a public voice" (Wieder, 2004, p. 23). Wieder (2004) situated his discussion
of testimony in the post-apartheid South African context of the Truth and Rec-
onciliation Commission and the power of the testimony from the "2,000 people
[who] publically testified and the 20,000 written statements" (p. 23). Testimony
as a form of oral life history rejects "modernist notions of rational autonomous
subjects, totalizing discourses, and foundationalist epistemologies" and, as such,
creates space to move past the privileging of whiteness and toward the act of
deconstructing whiteness (Tierney, 2003, p. 294).

Testimony has been characterized as "any retrospective account by the individual of his life in whole or part, in written or oral form, that has been elicited
or prompted by another person" (Watson & Watson-Franke, 1985, p. 2). Testimonial interview research is not intended to establish absolute truths or make
overgeneralized claims from the testimony of one respondent but rather becomes
a living history by which the person giving testimony, and the reader, can use
their own knowledge and experiences to evaluate the substance of the testimony.
In the case of whiteness, white racial identity has largely remained a theoretical
construct. While Bonilla-Silva (2006) has given empirical understanding to
some aspects of white racial identity theory, particularly color-blindness, little
empirical research exists. The method of testimonial research provides necessary
empirical data by which the theoretical framework of white racial identity can be
examined, particularly by educators. To this extent, the analysis of data derived
from testimony serves as one analytic lens of the data while simultaneously
providing space for readers to make their own evaluations and judgments. "No
two individuals engage time in the same manner," and each individual's interpretation of the testimony will be tempered against his or her own knowledge
and history in time, and thus create conclusions based on the evidence provided
in the testimony (Frank, 1995, p. 255). Similar to juror deliberations, each reader
of the proposed work will have a unique interaction with the testimonial data.

My analysis, findings, and discussion in ensuing chapters highlight beliefs
about this study's testimonial data, using the lenses by which I make sense of
the world and being based on my own experiences. To this extent, the method of
testimonial research used in this study specifically, and in my work more generally, has potential to provide a text that will stand over time, as the data can be
analyzed continually against sets of different experiential lenses. Testimony as

oral history creates an "on record" space through the power of participants' own language to better understand the epistemologies that either help or hinder participants' own understandings of their white racial identity development (Brown & Levinson, 1987; Tierney, 2003).

Interviews

To achieve a testimonial interview approach, research participants were interviewed twice using life history questions. The first interview explored the participants' general life experiences including information about where they grew up, their family and friends, the types of schools they attended and teachers they encountered, their choices about school and career, questions about why they chose to be educators, and how their beliefs are important in shaping their pedagogical decisions. The questions were designed to allow research participants to address areas of their identity without leading or prompting from the interviewer. The basic interview protocol was allowed flexibility since life history takes unexpected directions with respect to follow up questions.

The overall purpose of the first interview was establish a base sense of each participants' identity as she or he understood that identity and to help present each participant's case. The interview questions were neutral with respect to language about race and identity difference. Follow-up questions during the first interview were asked only to clarify information.

The second interview occurred two to three weeks after the first interview had been fully transcribed and had been shared with participants to ensure accuracy. One purpose of the second interview was to re-view major life history events (i.e., school, friends, family, career choice, pedagogical decisions, etc.) with overtly racialized language markers inserted into the questions. Again, the participants were free to testify and respond to the interview questions, and follow-up questions were asked to clarify information.

A secondary purpose of the subsequent interview was to look for both areas of consistency and discrepancy when racialized markers are present in the questions, as opposed to the racially neutral language of the first interview. In doing this, we are able to understand the discursive dialogic positions taken by participants with the presence of race as opposed to its absence. The second interviews were all fully transcribed as well and again shared with participants to check for accuracy.

Auto-ethnographic Data

Jones (2006) calls for making auto-ethnographic research and narratives explicit. In examining my own white racial identity, I am able to name the ways in which racism operates in my own life whereas much of the scholarship on whiteness is unable to do the same. The critique of McIntosh's famous knapsack of privilege has been the vagueness of what she identifies as privileges (McWhorter, 2005). To be specific and create disturbance, I subscribe to Nudd, Schriver, and Galloway's (2001) call to "to be implicated" in the texts that I create, as opposed to minimizing my responsibility for racism.

To be clear, I do not suggest that I write autobiography, as autobiography presents simple narrative vistas of events and benchmarks in one's life (Krieger, 1996). By using auto-ethnographic data as an epistemologically connected method, I draw on Reed-Danahay's (1997) conceptualization of auto-ethnography as a simultaneous questioning of the "realist conventions and objective observer position of standard ethnography" and engagement with questioning "the notion of [a] coherent, individual self" (p. 2). Inherent in this method is a critical gaze in which I use catalyst experiences and moments with race, racism, white supremacy, and racial identity in my own life to illuminate the standpoint by which I arrived at certain conclusions and analyses, and the way in which my life trajectory prohibits me from seeing and understanding a great deal about race. By engaging with auto-ethnography as a method, I argue that the larger analytical work of the research project has the potential to become more trustworthy (Denzin, 1989; Denzin & Lincoln, 2000, 2003a, 2003b, 2003c) as I situate the way in which my angle of vision to the world is linked with my own epistemological undergirding.

Participants

The nine participants who completed the research process were second-semester juniors at Righteous College. I provide here a very brief biological sketch of each participant as a means of introduction and to provide a sense of each participant. Listed alphabetically, participant names are pseudonyms to protect participant identity, except for me as I use my given name throughout the text.

Angela
Angela was a twenty year old who grew up in a rural agricultural community and attended a public K–12 school. Angela describes herself as having a small friendship group comprised of one best friend and other acquaintances. Angela is self-described as shy and quiet yet believes she is the most outgoing of her friends and was an active member of her high school drama club.

Barbara
When first asked about potential pseudonyms for this research project Barbara said, "Can I be called Fun Girl?" Barbara was twenty-one years old and spent most of her formative years moving around the country, spending school-aged time in an elite suburban area near Lilac, as well as an elite suburban area near Charleston, South Carolina, and in a suburban community in Mississippi; she

attended public schools in all three states. Barbara returned to Lilac to complete her undergraduate education. Because of the various moves, Barbara did not really articulate much about friendship circles or being close to peers.

Bob
Bob was a twenty year old who grew up in a rural community in the Northeast. Bob attended schools in his hometown public schooling system. Growing up, Bob was a student labeled with special needs and assigned to resource room support. Bob repeatedly reported throughout the interviews that his friends were the athletes in school, and he used narrative to create distance from kids who were not athletes, as if to be clear with me he was not like non-athletes.

Brian
Brian was a twenty year old who grew up in a middle-class suburb of the capital in the state where Righteous College is located. Brian attended private elementary and middle schools and then went to a suburban public high school. Brian did not talk much about friendships but did share closeness with his brother.

Cathy
Cathy was twenty years old and grew up approximately three hours from Righteous College in a small, rural suburb of a small industrial city. Cathy attended K–12 public schools. There are teachers in her extended family, and an uncle is a principal. Cathy does not have great memories of school; one of her first memories of school was being retained a grade in elementary school.

Kenny
Kenny, the researcher for this project, grew up and taught in the Lilac area. I came from a working-class and low socio-economic background. I attended public schools for K–8 and then went to a private high school. I taught in public schools in both an urban and a suburban setting.

Pat
Pat was a twenty-one year old who comes from a medium-sized suburb near a small urban area about seventy-five miles from Righteous College. Pat attended K–12 public schools. She graduated from high school with a class of eight hundred.

Sierra
Sierra was twenty-six and in her eighth contiguous year of undergraduate education; she spent time at Righteous College, went to a technical university, and then returned to Righteous College. Sierra grew up in a small city often characterized as socio-economically depressed and some two hours from the Righteous campus. Sierra briefly attended a suburban elementary school before moving into the city and attending public city schools in her area.

Steven
Steven was nineteen years old. Steven lived and attended public schools in a small "university city" that is home to a large Ivy League university. Steven's parents were both educators; his mother was president of the local teachers' union.

Todd
Todd was twenty-one years old and came from a suburban community approximately a five-hour drive from Righteous College. Todd's community was located about thirty minutes from the largest metropolitan area of the state, which was also one of the largest metropolitan areas in the country. Todd attended private Catholic schools for his entire K–12 schooling experience.

Data Analysis

As a qualitative researcher, I am concerned with representation and attention to analysis that seeks to understand. Lincoln and Guba (1985) remind me that interpretations "are likely to be meaningful for different realties" (p. 42). Case study has often been falsely understood as a product of qualitative research as opposed to an analytical process distinct from a product (Stake, 1995). In other words, case study has been commonly understood as the writing product of research itself, as opposed to a method of analyzing and ultimately writing data. My research approach and process use cases to better reflect the testimonial nature of the participants' interviews, rather using a written research product with the analytical focus on each person.

Focus on the particular has historically been given "less than full regard" in qualitative research (Denzin, 1989; Yin, 1989). Despite an orientation in qualitative research that gives less regard to the particular, case study analyses of the particular in one's testimony may serve to typify common occurrences over multiple sets or cases of testimony, leading to generalization-producing analysis. To this extent, a more glocal approach that honors the specific in each case (the local) and an understanding across cases (the more global) is achieved and the "case study can be seen as a small step toward grand generalization" (Stake, 1995, p. 141).

In approaching the interviews for this study with the case approach, I was able to gather data from individuals while looking more holistically at the data during the analysis phase, and also was able to propose findings that I believe capture cross-case coherence. My intent is to avoid Stake's (1995) critique of case study as being framed all too often as a product of research and not the form of inquiry itself. The research data gathered from the testimonial interviews and the document analysis of each participant were analyzed using the concept of case so that each case could be understood for what it had to offer.

Recognizing the case as a bounded system (Stake, 1995) whereby identity and explanation can be explored serves as the base for my analysis and for the findings that result from the analysis (White, 1992). The analysis provided by case study, as well as phenomena exhibited in the cases related to identity, serve as "cultural representation[s] and as sociological text" whereby narrative inquiry itself becomes a perspectival analytic tool (Clandinin & Connelly, 2004; Ellis & Bochner, 1996). In other words, the cases represent my researcher analytic decision making with the full acknowledgment that readers will extend the analysis based on their own experiences; each case study captures a perspective of the partial story testified to by the participants with the goal of integrated cross-case findings (Stake, 1995).

Coding

After the testimonial interviews were conducted, transcribed, and given an initial reading and analysis, an open coding system using colored pencils/markers was used to highlight constructs that were apparent across cases, or that seemed to typify constructs presented in the theoretical frameworks of white racial identity and critical race theory that guide this work. The colors were separated and analytical categories were developed based on consistencies with the data in particular color sets. The analytical categories, or emergent themes, that derived from the coding were explored, and are presented, explained, and instantiated with the data that forms the rest of this book.

Credibility

Lincoln and Guba (1985, 1989) highlight the importance in qualitative research for the process and the product to reflect a sense of credibility to think of a work as trustworthy. While many approaches have been undertaken to ensure credibility in research, Denzin and Lincoln (2003a, 2003b, 2003c) as well as Lincoln and Guba (1985,1989) propose the concept of member checking as a form of triangulation that helps give credibility to the research. Member checking involves participants' reviewing data to ensure that it accurately reflects what was said. In the case of the testimonial interviews for this study, the research participants received full transcriptions of their interviews and had the opportunity to read the transcripts and to query when they thought the transcription did not accurately reflect what was said. To further ensure credibility for any queries or discrepancies with the transcript, I played the audio recording of the interview for participants while we both looked at the transcription. This technique resulted in all participants' agreeing that the transcription was an accurate and honest reflection of the testimony provided. The member checking provided in this study ensured credibility and that the data was not invented or added by the researcher/transcriber (Denzin & Lincoln, 2003a, 2003b, 2003c; Lincoln & Guba, 1985, 1989). Because the participants had the opportunity to correct errors in the testimonial record, the basis by which the analysis was conducted and the findings that were generated derive from an uncontested set of texts. The sense of credibility provided in this study is important given that readers of the testimonial research are likely to reach conclusions informed by their own understandings, experiences, and readings of the text; the goal of establishing credibility is not to diminish the possibility for alternative or rival findings but rather to ensure that the data analyzed and presented is accurate so as to enhance readers' ability to seek out and argue alternate and rival findings (Patton, 1990).

A Note on the Presentation of Findings

My approach for the presentation of this book's findings looks at instantiations within participant interviews and uses participant testimonial data to warrant the assertions made. From the outset, I wish to be clear that the findings are not intended to be a focus merely on individual responses, but, rather, I intend that the findings present the individual responses as informative of the constructs across participant cases. The critique often lodged in work that examines race is that the evidence for particular findings is often unwarranted, speculative, and intuitive, so-called soft knowledge. While I understand that such critique is a defensive shield intended to protect the nature of whiteness, I nonetheless appreciate that such critiques will be made and am hopeful that my approach serves to preemptively address those critiques. I present multiple individual participant responses from across the sample to fully warrant my assertions within each finding. My findings are data rich with direct quotations from participant interviews across cases in making assertions and presenting findings, and do not rely on a softer claim/warrant presentation or a singular example from the data.

A potential tension between individual and group orientations also arises from my approach. If the unit of analysis were only to address individual participants at the level of their individual responses, findings could be easily dismissed as being the products and revelation of individual perspectives without connectivity. In a sense, there would be no findings at all but rather the presentation of nine individual representations of people who happened to participate in an interview study. To that extent, I employed a glocal (Wellman, 2002) approach, whereby individual responses (the local) serve to illuminate illustrative findings across the cases (the more global), shifting focus away from any one individual participant as "good/bad," "racist/non-racist," and so on, and opening the dialogue about the findings in a more expansive way; this represents what I have suggested to be "case as analysis" as opposed to "case as product" (Bonilla-Silva, 2006; Eliasoph, 1997).

On Findings and Discussion

Chapters 4, 5, and 6 present the findings that emerged from several layers of data analysis and discussion. The first finding presented in chapter 4 is that participants appeared to demonstrate a propensity toward the use of what Bonilla-Silva (2006) calls "semantic moves" when speaking about race and beliefs relative to race (p. 57). In exploring this finding, two sub-findings related to participant discourse arose: participants engaged in white racial bonding as well as the use of color-blind discourse and rhetoric. Participants' approaches to color-blind discourse varied; primarily, participants used expansive language of inclusion and being non-judgmental while simultaneously positioning restrictive views of racial inferiority and presenting what Bonilla-Silva (2006) frames as abstract liberalism. To illustrate abstract liberalism, I present auto-ethnographic data to situate how my own experiences are similar replications of what participants presented throughout the interview process.

Less frequently, color-blind discourse was marked by minimization and naturalization of race. The color-blind framings of participants, regardless of type, often included confused language and conceptualizations of race that at times presented incoherent narratives. Discussion will center on how both sub-findings work in concert in the maintenance of whiteness' property value, and how the social structure by which white supremacy and subordination of minority groups occurs.

The second major finding in chapter 5 asserts that participants did not demonstrate complex explanations of their rationales to be teachers; they often focused on surface-level reasons and cliché orientations to the profession that could be viewed as being naïve. In discussing this finding, I place some focus on the long-term effects of under-developed rationales of pre-service teachers once they have left the program and how the finding contributes to the education debt. Specifically, attention is placed on how the finding reflects yet another semantic move made by participants relative to race; as in the case of participants, this professional naïveté can block teachers from becoming culturally relevant and serves to exacerbate the potential to receive racially uninformed and poor instruction.

The third finding in chapter 6 is actually a set of amalgamated, smaller inter-related assertions relative to white racial identity, beginning with the ideas that (a) participants conceptualized diversity as analogous to race, unable to distinguish between the two constructs; (b) participants' understanding of their white identity was often linked by participants not to self but to "racial others;" and, finally, (c) participants' white racial identity was often presented with incoherence and in under-developed ways. In this finding, I present additional auto-ethnographic data to help situate my own white racial identity. Based on the revelations of previous participants' data, and specific responses within the smaller assertions relative to white racial identity, I present where I believe all participants are located in the Helms (1984, 1990, 2003) White Racial Identity model.

After locating each participant within the WRI model, I argue that the Helms WRI model appears to be a limited analytic in moving forward the discussion about race and racism. I suggest that given the model's propensity for placing participants within an individualistic orientation to racial identity, the model ignores the systematic nature of white privilege and whiteness that confers benefits to whites beyond the level of isolated individuals. Further, I argue that the model does not account for what participants both choose not to reveal and what they in fact do not know about themselves. Through discussion, I offer a different model for exploring WRI that addresses both the nature of the individual and the system of white supremacy that confers privileges on whites as a connected group of individuals.

Chapter 4
Semantic Moves Relative to Race

For the purposes of my discussion, semantic moves can be understood as any utterance, linguistic construction, or assertion used in the process of signifying (Hall, 1997) or otherwise demarking an idea within a communication framework. While our beliefs about any number of constructs can be maintained privately, it is through linguistic utterances, or semantic moves, that we begin to understand how people frame their beliefs. Throughout the interviews conducted for this research, pre-service teacher participants used a variety of semantic moves and rhetorical constructions to discuss race (Bonilla-Silva, 2001). Embedded within the narrative responses to questions, participants expressed views, ideas, and beliefs about race using a variety of semantic moves. These semantic moves varied from expressions of white racial bonding to a variety of color-blind approaches (Bonilla-Silva 2001, 2006). Each of the semantic moves will be explored in this chapter.

White Racial Bonding

The first semantic move that the participating pre-service teachers demonstrated was the use of racial bonding through discourse structures. That pre-service teachers engaged in white racial bonding indicates that while white pre-service teachers may not be apt to outline what white is on record (Brown & Levinson, 1987) to a general public, they do have a sense of what whiteness is. When one engages in white racial bonding, her or his sense of whiteness leads to a bonding relationship with others who are believed to share the property value of white-ness (Harris, 1995) in the comfort and safety of whiteness' shelter.

I remember a conversation regarding "slang" the first time I taught a linguistics course. Several white students were upset that they did not understand the slang of particular groups and thought that it was unfair that they could not understand what was being communicated. Two ideas emerged in our conversation: (1) the exclusionary nature of slang was only a problem when "other" people use it, and (2) the students in my class also used a slang of their own that was a means to express shared values and knowledge to the exclusion of groups not meant to be the beneficiaries of that shared knowledge. This principle of including white people within a particular belief of shared knowledge, while excluding those who are not white from the full implications of the shared knowledge, organizes the concept of white racial bonding through the particular discourse structures.

"You know:" the language marker most often used to denote white racial bonding by this study's participants. Eight of the nine participants used the exact phrase "you know" during the interview process. While each individual participant accomplished a different purpose with their deployment of "you know," all of the uses ultimately centered on establishing shared knowledge between them and me around whiteness, specifically, and race, generally, representing a level of racial bonding. Brian, for example, used the phrase "you know" to dismiss the concept that whiteness could affect a teacher's way of teaching, specifically asserting that whiteness does not play a role; instead, Brian said it is "where they grew up, you know," attributing differences in teaching style to the geography of one's experiences rather than to one's whiteness.

Bob, on the other hand, used the phrase "you know" to establish bonding around levels of discomfort with what white people should call other groups, saying, "The first time I ever saw, uhh, you know (dip in voice), African American students, (raises voice back) you know." Bob's dip in voice highlighted a discomfort in how to frame his first experience with students from different racial backgrounds. His use of "you know" to ground his description suggested that as a fellow white person, I would understand the difficulty in framing others, hence becoming a shared value of our whiteness despite the fact that Bob knew relatively little about me, generally, and certainly knew nothing of my personal experiences with difference.

Angela's approach to the use of "you know" was still a different semantic approach to articulating bonding in that Angela established that she would never know what it was like to be from the non-dominant racial group, and her use of "you know" helped to establish that, as a white person. I too must understand her dilemma. Angela said, "I will never have the experience of being a Black racial person minority or majority or anything, you know." In this conceptualization, Angela established that I too am white, and consequently never will have the experience of being non-white. Thus, from her perspective we had a means of bonding.

Cathy, on the other hand, bonded based on the lessons parents teach children. When asked what she learned about other groups of people, Cathy asserted, "You know, don't judge anyone till you get to know them." While Cathy did not know me, her assumptions, represented in the use of "you know," were aimed at how we might share the socialization of being non-judgmental.

Still other participants used the phrase "you know" to establish shared judgment of groups of people of color. In response to an interview question about student behavior, Todd asserted, "I know some of the kids didn't have the best parents, you know." Todd was not alone as many of the participants used what they believed to be a shared value that parents of minority students were not the best parents. Todd's particular use of "you know" helped to establish what he thought was a shared understanding of poor parenting.

Todd further used the concept of "you know" in bonding to establish with me as the researcher that he did not have negative thoughts about Black teachers. When asked if he had ever had Black teachers, Todd responded, "I don't think twice about it, and it's not something that I take into account, and if you see the teacher is Black I'm not like ohhh, and I am not, you know, I had Jones and Smith (both Black faculty) and I don't have any preconceptions of them." The answer Todd provided did not relate directly to the question asked, but did establish that Todd wanted to share a bond with me, whereby I would understand that he did not judge a teacher's race or somehow that the race does not even enter his consciousness. Interestingly, Todd did not finish the statement, indicating that I already understood what he was saying and the meaning to his response; consequently there was no need to continue responding.

Sierra also used the phrase "you know" to establish judgments about groups that must be shared knowledge among white people. Sierra asserted that her hometown "is becoming more diverse, uhmm, there are two maximum security prisons, and, you know, (then mumbles) how prison populations are mostly Black." Sierra assumed that I would recognize prison populations to be mostly Black, and that the population of prisoners was what established her community as diverse.

In describing "bad kids," Pat stated, "More now that I have taken education classes, you know, it's home life." While I did not teach Pat in the diversity course, I was familiar with the syllabus of the instructor who did teach the course, and my perception was that Pat was not taught that negative student behavior is a result of home life. Yet, Pat believed that she learned this concept in her diversity course; she also believed that as a fellow white person, and a faculty member who taught the course as well, I would see that student behavior is linked to home life.

The phrase "you know" in and of itself does not reveal to be inherently problematic at a purely linguistic level. As a general statement, "you know" is linguistically benign. What is problematic are the ways in which participants used the phrase and the location of the semantic move for insertion into responses that demarcate a bonding experience along lines of race. I argue that in using the phrase "you know," participants attempted to highlight that as a white person I must have a particular shared insight into what was being said. In the first iterations of data analysis (there were five iterations in all—transcription, member checking, coding, sorting, and cross-case analysis) I was concerned that perhaps the use of "you know" was language filler and linguistically benign as previously suggested. I thought that the phrase might have been used by participants as a non-significant marker of nerves or uncertainty with how to answer a question. In fact, when one documents the cases of each participant as layers of data analysis, the phrase of "you know" does not overwhelm or dominate any one participant's experience in the interview and, as stand-alone cases, is not significant.

After a review of the data, however, over multiple layers of analysis, and a close examination of the occurrence of "you know" within the context of the interviews across participant cases, a pattern emerged. Participants' use of "you know" occurred only directly before, during, or directly after participants used language and description that could be viewed as polemical or "loaded," to the extent that the language exhibited high levels of judging non-white groups and/or indicated struggle with concepts related to race. The use of "you know" did not appear to be part of the participants' regular discourse patterns during the interviews. Had the pattern appeared in other aspects of participant discourse, in a regular pattern of utterances, for example, we might assume that the phrase met the condition of being linguistically benign. Rather, the occurrences, as they played out in the participants' narratives, appear to present as a semantic move and linguistic tool used to establish affinity and bonding between the white participants and me as a fellow white.

In the instances where the "you know" phrase was invoked by participants, there was an attempt to establish that what was being asserted was shared and common knowledge, and thus I would know and consequently understand the assertions being made. This idea that the knowledge being discussed could be a shared value seems to indicate a relative connection premised on our race given that I was not known to the participants prior to speaking with them. I argue that if the participants in this project had perceived me to be racially different from them, they would not have used the phrase "you know," as they would not necessarily have believed that the information they were saying was of shared value. Consequently, participants would not necessarily have felt "safe" in expressing some of their positions, views, and beliefs with someone whom they saw as racially other.

The use of "you know" is much more than a semantic move to express bonding; it is a semantic move that shows white people feel safe in revealing ideas that non-white groups may see as problematic within intragroup contexts. An instantiation is Pat's assertion of "you know," for example, to explain what she perceived as bad home life. The establishment of "you know" makes sense only given participants' perceived affinity to me as a fellow white person. If participants had perceived me to be non-white, or not valuing whiteness' property value – a race-traitor (Ignatiev, 1995) for example – their narrative responses to questions would have inherently and necessarily discounted my ability to share in the same personal property affirmed to white people vis-à-vis whiteness' value; thus there would have been no need or utility in the discourse of shared knowledge that "you know" creates.

Color-Blind Orientations to Race

In the post *Brown v. Board of Education of Topeka* (1954) United States, many white people have internalized that on-record (Brown & Levinson, 1987) discriminatory, and racist comments are not acceptable forms of discourse. In establishing a rationality for their beliefs, many white people mark outwardly racist comments as the product of irrational racist people such as skin-heads, Klu Klux Klan members, Nazis, neo-Nazis, and other groups or individuals that may hold beliefs outside of the mainstream despite how they present themselves; Glenn Beck and Rush Limbaugh are examples (Bonilla-Silva, 2006, 2001). In creating distance from these so-called irrational racists, many white people have developed other forms of discourse or semantic moves to communicate racialized beliefs. Bonilla-Silva (2006) highlights that color-blind racism, a form of post-Brown "racism lite," is one semantic move used by white people to protect views of race that are in fact racist in nature.

Bonilla-Silva (2006, 2003, 2001), Williams (1997), Leonard (2004), Thompson (2003), and Ferber (2003) have all explored the nature of color-blind racism in their work. Bonilla-Silva (2006, 2001) moves forward a framework for understanding color-blind racism through the identification of several components or constructs where color-blind racism manifests. The four major constructs are an abstract liberalism with conflicts to the liberal articulations, biologization, naturalization, and minimization (Bonilla-Silva, 2006). While Bonilla-Silva's framework has been significant in the larger body of race research, exploring how the framework plays out against empirical educational data such as teacher participant interviews is a unique angle of vision on understanding color-blind racism. Drawing from my corpus of data in presenting the sub-finding relative to color-blindness, I suggest that and explain how these components of color-blind discourse were very much present in the narratives of the pre-service teacher participants.

Abstract Liberalism

By far, the largest and most significant manifestation of color-blind discourse was through what has been conceptualized as abstract liberalism. The concept of abstract liberalism is an engagement with ideas that reflect liberal ideals, both political and economic, to explain race while simultaneously engaging in discourse that often conflicts with these liberal views and reveals a far more conservative orientation to race (Bonilla-Silva, 2006). Drawing from the Critical Race Theory concept of expansive versus restrictive approaches to race, I suggest that participants engaged the articulation of surface-level beliefs and commitments that appeared to be expansive (liberal) but actually covered beliefs that were restrictive (conflicts to liberal ideology). In other words, what white people actually believe is not expressed in what white people directly say.

Crenshaw (1995), Tate and Rousseau (2002), and Dixson and Rousseau (2005) all discussed the role of expansive versus restrictive constructions of race. The expansive view of anti-discrimination policies conceives of ending the conditions and circumstances by which the subordination of Black people exists, working "to further the national goal for eradicating the effects of racial oppression" vis-à-vis the casting of a broad net (Crenshaw, 1995, p. 105). On the other hand, restrictionists pose that discriminatory acts take place in isolation, are targeted at individuals, and are not representative of policies targeted to whole groups (Crenshaw, 1995; Dixson & Rousseau, 2004). To this extent, restrictionists are sheltered from dealing with race outside of very narrowly constructed, localized, and historical experiences or contexts and thus are unable to lodge racial critiques.

An excellent contemporary example of expansive and restrictive tension can be found in the John G. Roberts-led Supreme Court decision in the case of *Ricci et al. v. DeStefano et al.* (2009). Written by conservative justice Anthony Kennedy and signed onto by justices John G. Roberts, Samuel Alito, Clarence Thomas, and Antonin Scalia (the other conservative justices of the Roberts court), this majority opinion legislated from the bench created more restrictive approaches to dealing with anti-discrimination. In debating the nomination of justice Sonia Sotomayor, conservative pundits feared that she would legislate from the bench to promote expansive ideals that could be in conflict with current law. The irony in the Supreme Court's decision in the *Ricci* case is that, in fact, it legislates. In overturning the lower court's decision, which was affirmed in part by the appeals court on which Sotomayor sat, the court legislated against the current law to protect white interests in restrictionist ways. In the wake of the 2009 decision, many legal scholars believe that the federal appellate court panel, of which Sotomayor was a part, properly followed law and adhered to Title VII rights in this case, certainly as addressed by the dissenting opinion of the justices of the time Ruth Bader Ginsburg, David Souter, John Paul Stevens, and Stephen Breyer.

The Kennedy opinion makes it more difficult for minority applicants and minority employees to pursue litigation for discrimination under Title VII legislation, reducing employment discrimination to complex individual instantiations. The Court's majority opinion articulated a common restrictionist stance by dismissing the New Haven Fire Department's proactive attempt to address racial inequity by not promoting white firefighters when it was found that the promotion test and the results of the promotion test adversely affected minority applicants. In her dissenting opinion, Ginsburg asserted that the white firefighters had nothing taken away from them; they were not given preference nor did they have preference withheld. Thus, no loss occurred, and further, the firefighters were not inherently entitled to anything. In the Court's majority opinion, Justice Kennedy used expansive liberal-sounding ideology of "fairness" and "equality" to give the white firefighters, an already over-represented group, an avenue of redress, while applying restrictionist doctrine to prevent the minority firefighters, in this case, or minority employees and applicants in general, to seek relief and redress from the court.

In the case of this study's participants, a similar approach to the Supreme Court's majority writing surfaces with respect to color-blind orientations. Participants often attempted to claim, and initially establish, a non-racist expansive liberal identity but then followed up their discourse with conflicts to the much-purported non-racist, non-judgmental identity that was far more restrictive in nature. In coming to terms with these conflicting positions, participants engaged in the abstract liberalism form of color-blind discourse, and also displayed a great deal of confusion relative to race.

Establishment of Non-racist, Color-Blind, Expansive Standpoints

Respondents used a variety of techniques to establish non-racist, non-judgmental, open, and expansive positions. When asked what she was taught about other groups of people, Angela, asserted, "Be nice to everybody" and "My family is big on don't judge, never judge, you never pass judgment." Similarly, Cathy asserted, "My parents for the most part they always said you know don't judge." Todd and Steven also engaged in a similar narrative; Todd responded that he learned "that you can't judge anyone," and Steven asserted that he learned "never [to be] biased." Brian used a slightly different tack in responding, the "thou shall not judge" approach, asserting that his beliefs are that "pretty much everyone is equal and I have never really thought of me being special or more gifted than anybody." Barbara articulated one of the most cliché forms of abstract liberalism, saying, "My mom always raised me not to see skin color"; seemingly Barbara could literally be blinded to the existence of race. Barbara furthermore claimed, "We are not (four second pause)—we are very accepting and are not judgmental or discriminatory." Barbara did not finish her initial thought of what her family is not; rather, she first paused and then established that she is accepting, but did go on to further assert not being "judgmental or discriminatory."

When asked about his friendship circle and the friendship circle of his family, Brian quickly moved to establish a non-racist, non-judgmental identity. Brian said,

> I think everyone in my family was pretty much white but I had a lot of different friends growing up because I played basketball, African American friends, and we were all one big community and we weren't a racist bunch (laughs awkwardly). It's like everything was everything and I didn't see them for their skin color and it wasn't said I think it wasn't talked about but you just kind of knew.

In this one complex statement, Brian attempted to establish that, from a liberal perspective, he is not racist. He asserted "We weren't a racist bunch," and despite laughing awkwardly about his own statement, claiming not to see his friends for their skin color, thus demonstrating an evidently color-blind approach. In his statement he also established his African American friends as "them," clearly distinguishing "them" from "him," concretely contradicting his assertion that he did not see them for race. To confirm the contradiction in his narrative, Brian ended with the idea that race was present, something "you just kind of knew" but that "wasn't talked about." In not talking about it but knowing it, Brian established that to maintain an expansive perspective or standpoint on race, white people must be able to hold in what they know without saying it out loud.

Bob also enacted a "now-you-see-it, now-you-don't" approach in attempting to establish a liberal open belief system of being non-judgmental, while simultaneously narrating a discourse full of contradictions. When asked about his friendship circle and that of his family, and if the friendship group included people other than white people, Bob said,

> No. We kind of growing up with who was around and we didn't really know anyone around, and I do know my dad has played beer league softball and there was a Black guy on there and he was friends with him and they live kind of close. They are always friendly and they have always raised me not to judge people by any means even in school there was only a couple of them, and I was always friends with all of them, and I always had them come over, and, like, that and never had a problem and they raised me to be, but just the location did not allow it.

In the narrative Bob established that he was raised "not to judge people by any means," creating the space to claim an expansive identity, but he did have several contradictions. In one instance, Bob implied that he was friends with "who was around" and that he "didn't really know anyone around," yet Bob also asserted that there was a Black family that lived close by and that his dad knew at least someone who was Black and they were friendly. Simultaneously, Bob claimed that he was friends with "them" which in the context of the narrative "them" could signify only non-white friends, even though he previously stated that "no," the friendship circle did not include people who were not white. In his last statement, Bob said that "they," his parents, "raised me to be," and based on the context of the previous statements, we understand that his parents raised him to be non-judgmental, but geography, "the location," was the reason that "did not allow it," meaning that geography did not allow him to be non-judgmental. Bob's narrative is complex, and though he attempted primarily to establish a non-racist, non-judgmental, and expansive identity, Bob also brought a number of contradictions to the narrative. In the next section, I will present a number of contradictions to the abstract liberal ideology exposé that helps to locate the nature of conflict between the expansive standpoint and the restrictive views endemic to color-blind racism through abstract liberalism.

Conflicts to Abstract Liberal, Non-judgmental Narratives

The seven participants (Angela, Barbara, Bob, Brian, Cathy, Steven, and Todd) in the study who attempted to establish outwardly abstract liberal, non-judgmental, and expansive standpoints also had conflicts with such an epistemological standpoint on race that in part highlight the very nature of abstract liberalism as a color-blind discourse. Whereas Brian previously said he had been taught not to judge, in his answer to the next interview question about some of his experiences growing up that might have indicated he was white, Brian commented about basketball,

> We always play teams from inner-city Connecticut or Lilac and you would be like WOW! we are really white and they would come in and the pants are down and they got shorts that are too long and you're looking like ohhh OK, just the way they talked and interacted was different than us, and growing up you flipped to BET and you would see that and be like, this is not my life at all. I had it good compared to a lot of people out there.

In his previous statement, Brian had asserted that "everyone is equal," yet his narrative revealed something entirely different. In fact, Brian made numerous judgments, and, despite his claim that he never thought of himself as "being more special" than anyone, he clearly indicated that his life and experiences were in fact better than others, as exhibited in his statement, "I had it good compared to a lot of people." Brian's use of "WOW! we are really white" and "looking like ohhh, OK" also established his judgments and supported that his perception of the other basketball players was based on race, his judgments of race, and his establishment that he was different from the inner-city players.

Barbara used geography as a means to literally claim to not see race, asserting that she was "very accepting" and "not judgmental or discriminatory" when discussing where she wanted to teach. Barbara asserted, "I would like to teach down South, only because I would be beneficial there because I am the radical New Yorker in the Christian Bible thumper southern belt." In her statement Barbara highlighted that she did have judgments of people based on both their geography and their religious orientation; in her framing of people being "in the Christian Bible thumper southern belt," Barbara established a superiority to said people by being the "radical New Yorker," and that she would in fact be "beneficial" to students because of her superior position. Barbara's use of geography as a proxy for race and religion complicated and challenged her previous rhetoric that she was not judgmental.

Bob, who previously had conflicts between his desired expansive presentation and his restrictive standpoints, continued throughout his second interview to engage in judgmental language as Barbara did. When asked if he had ever had teachers who were not white, Bob responded, "I always had white teachers. I only had one Native American teacher, but maybe I shouldn't say that 'cause she is from India." In a follow-up session, I asked Bob what the experience was like having a teacher from a different race from him and Bob said, "Uhm *you know* it was [a] little, I didn't know, I mean she looked a little different and she kind of talked a little bit weird." Whereas Bob earlier had professed that his orientation was around not judging people, he first displayed a confusion of the teacher's race altogether and then framed her as looking "a little different" and talking "a little bit weird," both judgmental perspectives inconsistent with his self-proclaimed, non-judgmental, and expansive self-positioning.

Bob also carried his judgments into how he framed students. When asked if students from underrepresented groups need different types of instruction than white peers, Bob's answer revealed how he in fact judged students of color. Bob asserted,

> Uhmm, I just think *you know* you have to be more patient with them . . . they just don't want to learn, be in school, *you know*, they don't want to be in school. That's why they're always late to class and have excuses.

In this piece of narrative, Bob talked about students of color, in block, using pathological and judgmental conceptions. Bob made assumptions about and also laid down judgments about students' desire to be in school, and their motivation to learn, and he used what he perceived to be an aversion to school on the part of students of color, to justify what he framed and believed about students of color being "always late to class" and having "excuses."

Bob's socialization to the profession seemed to have done the work of confirming his judgmental beliefs for him. Bob claimed to have an interest in teaching in an urban setting, and when talking about his field placement experience in an urban setting, Bob said, "I have been to those schools before and they just screw around and dick around," and then talking about his particular placement at an open school called School Absent of Structures (SAS), Bob went on to say,

> It's all African Americans, and the kids come in and they are late, don't understand what's going on and the teacher came in and was really frustrated and he yelled at them and I laughed at him and I was like, where are you going at inner-city kids like that, you're going nowhere and they were giving him shit, he was white and he was frustrated.

To complete his thought about potentially teaching in the city, Bob said,

> I found I really don't care. I was really, like, I really like the inner-city 'cause I can show patience with these kids and there are some gambles and you have to give up some things, you can't be as strict with as normal but I saw

kids wearing an iPod doing examples...if he sits there and doing work that's
a great idea and so I'm kind of curious if I can handle it, so far I like it.

Bob's narrative has multiple layers and is quite complex. Previously, Bob had
claimed to have a non-judgmental identity, yet immediately, he asserted that he
knew what an urban setting was all about and that "they," his reference for in-
ner- city students of color, "just screw around and dick around." This judgment
was then reified for Bob when he was placed in an urban school, SAS, where he
correlated that the students are all "African American," "late," and "don't understand" what is going on. Bob recognized that yelling at children is probably not
an effective technique, but associated the fact that yelling is not effective because "where you going at inner-city kids like that," reducing the conversation
from critiquing the method of yelling at children, in general, to a focus only on
inner-city students. As Bob continued, his justification for being interested in
teaching in an urban setting was also predicated on judgments about children
that, as a teacher, "you can't be as strict as normal." The implication is that in a
non-inner-city setting, you can afford to be strict and, in turn, have higher standards. So Bob's desire to potentially teach in an inner-city setting ultimately was
derived from a curiosity about whether he "can handle it." The narrative Bob
used posits many judgments that all seem in contradiction to his self-positioning
in expansive ways.

Todd initially asserted that he was taught, "You can't judge anyone," and
continued from there to initiate discourse that seemed to border on judgments in
saying that his family "would never stereotype anyone as like Hispanic or African American or Italian and just very open minded." The corollary seems to be
that if you do not judge people, there appears to be no need to tell anyone the
specific groups you do not judge; being non-judgmental would assume to be in
all instances if the identity were truly non-judgmental. Conceptualizing the specifics of what would not happen in terms of stereotypes implies that Todd in fact
did have stereotypical conceptions of others that he recognized as not being
what he should do. Bonilla-Silva (2006) talks about the nature of color-blind
racism being a slippery conceptualization; even though Todd claims not to be
judgmental there is an implication around how Hispanics, African Americans, or
Italians can be stereotyped and thus were clearly a part of Todd's conscious,
even when he claimed not to be judgmental.

Todd used other judgmental language to conceptualize students. When
asked if students from under-represented groups need different instruction from
white peers, Todd said, "No, because like, I mean, any African American or
Latino can be just as smart as white kids and there will be African American or
Latino students that will be good students, and I don't like to generalize." Ironically, it is Todd's answer itself that puts forward generalizations about African
American and Latino students per the underlying assumptions in Todd's response, that generally students from minority backgrounds are not inherently as
smart as white kids but they "can be just as smart" and there "will be" students

from minority populations who can be "good students." Todd's narrative did not assert that African American and Latino students *are* as smart but rather they "can be," a judgment that revealed Todd's conceptualizations to be deeper than, and in conflict with, the assertion that he was not judgmental.

Steven articulated his conflicting beliefs relative to students' language and relative to his experiences with Black students and in deciding to attend Righteous College. When asked if students from under-represented groups needed different instruction from their white peers, Steven said,

> I guess there isn't a difference and it should be the same, I mean there is a language barrier but you might have to explain it more so they can fully explain it, but no they should all just get the same.

This statement itself is filled with contradiction. Steven front ended and back ended his thought with the expansive concept of a broad net being cast and that race should not affect the opportunities offered to students, that students from all races "should be the same" and "all just get the same." Between this framing, Steven articulated his belief, which stands in conflict to expansive orientations on race, by asserting definitely that there is a language barrier in place when dealing with students of color and that if teachers are not careful to explain things to students of color, the students will not get it.

Steven also revealed an interesting perspective about his beliefs in describing his football recruiting trip to Righteous College, saying, "I first came here for football and there was like six Black kids on the team and that was like, OK, this is weird." In finishing his story about the experience, Steven shared, "I got paired up with a Black kid on the football team but I got a sleepover with him and it didn't bother me or affect my decision." Having previously asserted that he had been taught "never being biased with anyone," Steven found that having six kids of color on the football team was "weird," an articulation of judgment. Further, Steven said that having a Black roommate did not "bother" him or "affect" his decision to attend Righteous. While saying that the experience did not do these things, Steven implied that having a Black roommate could have bothered him or affected his decision. In articulating the expansive, that the experience had no effect, he needed to tell the story in a way that positioned him in the expansive while also conceptualizing the presence of Black kids as "weird"; this revealed that the restrictive judgmental aspect of his beliefs was near in his mind and that he wanted to create open distance from them semantically.

Angela's judgments reveal themselves slightly differently from those of the other participants. While Angela did not use race outwardly as the basis for directly revealing her judgments, she did relegate her judgments more generally to the nature of families. When describing her belief of from where student behavior originates, Angela said kids "who didn't come from the best of families . . . like a lot of them were from foster care or came from families that where they didn't have socio-economic advantages and were down on their luck, kind of where things weren't valued." The nature of Angela's judgments were in direct conflict with her belief that you "don't judge, never judge, you never pass judgment." Angela conceptualized that families who are struggling are simultaneously families where "things weren't valued," displaying that, in fact, she did pass a high level of judgment.

Finally, Cathy also displayed a number of judgments that seemed to be in direct conflict with the idea that she was not judgmental. Cathy claimed that her parents taught her "don't judge" but followed up by claiming that non-judgment extends "even to kids they knew were not good kids." In Cathy's example, trying to place herself within the expansive arena of being non-judgmental says one should not judge the kids, even those who were not good kids. This statement is highly conflicting in nature and confusing, as the conceptualization of kids as not being good kids appears to reveal a judgment in direct conflict with how Cathy has framed herself and her family as non-judgmental.

Cathy revealed two other rather interesting conflicts relative to a non-judgmental perspective. First, even though Cathy had already asserted that she and her family were non-judgmental, she told a story that reveals a level of judgment about African Americans. Cathy said,

> My older cousin had an African American friend at college and he came to visit, and my grandma was all furious and not very happy about it and my cousin was trying to explain to her and she was just like, it's not what I'm used to, and then my brother persisted to call him the chocolate man because my grandmother said I had never seen a chocolate man before and she was like, they are a little bit different and so she was like, well there were certain things we would laugh about.

In this statement Cathy reveals that she was in fact socialized by a judgmental belief system even though she claimed that was not part of her experience. In particular, Cathy reveals that her grandmother showed fury that her cousin had an African American friend and that "they are a little bit different." The judgmental nature then carried over to her brother's conceptualization of the friend as a "chocolate man," and Cathy's finding the use of *chocolate man* to be a conceptualization containing humor. The humor that Cathy found came at the expense of her cousin's African American friend and ultimately was derived from judgmental conceptualizations.

Kenny in the Non-judgmental Judgment Conundrum

Like many of the participants, I too was taught at the surface not to judge, and that message was often reified directly before and after either parent would judge someone. I remember clearly one exchange from my childhood when I was at a grocery store with my mother. My mother was watching a Black woman using food stamp coupons to purchase steaks. When we got home, she phoned a girlfriend and began to complain about how "they" just needed to get work and not sit around all day, and why should she be responsible for providing for people like "them," and they have "the nerve" of purchasing steak. The exchange went on for some time, and even at a young age of probably six or seven I understood it as being racially charged. Once aware that I had heard the entire conversation, she admonished me, saying, "We don't judge people. That wasn't because she was Black; I just can't stand seeing people get something they don't deserve, but remember that it's not nice to judge." If the exchange was not really about the woman's race there would have been no need to add in race to what she was telling me. Further, front-loading and back-loading reminders not to judge prove interesting and ultimately reveal a mechanism whereby children are socialized to a particular discourse pattern of couching judgments in ideologically open frames. That exchange was typical of many exchanges within my family. The real message was never that we did not judge, but rather it was "do not get yourself caught judging other people outside the comfort of your friends and family." It was an experience of "keeping up appearances," a message made clear to me at an early age that judging is not the problem but, rather, having your judgments exposed is the problem. In my socialization experiences, my elders (beyond parents) often criticized any group unlike them, including people who were poorer than us, more financially secure than us, thinner than us, heavier than us, of different religious orientations, sexual orientations, and family configurations from us. "Us" was always the metric by which other groups were judged.

This judgment socialization has impacted my own interactions with people whose identities represent difference. While it might be pleasant to think that I am not judgmental, I know that I am and have to constantly remind myself that the judgments come from being socialized by white parents in a white (hetero)sexist, racist, classist, white supremacist society (hooks, 2003). My response to balancing what I know are judgmental orientations has often been what I call "hyper-extending", or going overboard and acting "extra" in my interactions with people different from me, in order to conceal my own judgmental nature. I was aware of what I call the hyper-extending in my late teens and early adulthood and recognize that it shaped friendship circles, interactions, and even job choices. I took my first teaching job in the city school district not necessarily because I wanted to work there, but to prove that I could work in the city without anyone's knowing what my judgments of the families and locations might be, despite having grown up in the same school district and having had similar judgments levied against my peers and me.

Naturalization

Naturalization, as a form of color-blind discourse, allows participants to justify perceived differences between races and the racism attached to white people's behavior as a naturally occurring phenomenon, a sort of "Just the way it is; what can I do?" approach to dealing with issues of race. Enacting upon a naturalization frame to organize one's color-blindness is a shift away from how abstract liberalism operates, where the speaker can attempt to self-frame as being non-judgmental as a precursor to her or his judgmental commentary. In naturalization, there is a casual recognition that racism exists and that is just the way it is. Participants Pat and Sierra used naturalization as their primary semantic move with respect to color-blindness, and Barbara used some naturalization in tandem with her abstract liberalism.

Pat recounted a story of middle school romance and how her learning a naturalization lesson then still framed some of her experiences with people of color. Whereas in the previous section we saw that seven of the participants claimed to have learned lessons in non-judgment from their families, Pat presented a discrepant narrative that located her within the space of naturalization of race. Pat said,

> I remember in sixth grade I had a crush on this African American kid and I was telling my mom about it and it was a life lesson that didn't pertain to sixth grade, and she told me she wouldn't have a problem with it but it would be my brothers, I have three older brothers, and my dad that would have a problem and we had a discussion about why would that matter and she gave me the speech about the interracial thing and how other people look at it and it's hard for me.

In this story Pat gave verbal confirmation of the way stock stories (Delgado, 1993) operate; Pat said that she received "the speech about the interracial thing," acknowledging that there was a master narrative about interracial relationships that white people can go to in socializing their children to the white/right way of thinking about particular race situations. In fact, Pat's mother seemed able to avoid engaging in her personal beliefs to enact this socialization, as she deferred responsibility for the racism to Pat's brothers and father. To some extent Pat's mother, vis-à-vis Pat's hearsay narrative, showed her own desire to situate herself within an abstract color-blind discourse pattern, while socializing Pat that the sermonic message of the stock story was valid and she should adhere to it. Pat ended the telling of this story by justifying the rationale for her brothers' and father's hypothetical need to protect her when she said, "I got angry, but it has to do a lot with me being the little girl and the only girl, and they are watching out." Through either her own beliefs or as a result of what was socialized to her in this naturalization experience, Pat relegated the issue of the racism as a natural consequence of something more important, her family protecting her. Pat did not sufficiently problematize the stance in her narrative, and given that this is what she reports as being the lesson she was taught about others from her family, the color-blind via naturalization approach had sufficient impact on Pat's racialized narratives.

Like Pat, Sierra gave insight into the naturalization of racial order that was socialized to her at a young age. While Sierra said that her mother was more open than her father, she described what she learned about others from her family during this exchange:

Kenny: What did your family teach you about other groups of people?
Sierra: Pretty much that white is right . . .

Kenny: . . . really, you remember that growing up . . .
Sierra: . . . yeah, my dad is pretty much an Archie Bunker type, if you ever date a Black person I'm disowning you and blah, blah, blah, my dad is pretty bigoted (laughs heartily).

Sierra's use of "blah, blah, blah" recognized her father's racist orientation as part of the stock story (Delgado, 1993) about warnings white parents give to their children about the consequences of interracial relationships, similar to Pat's conversation with her mother. Sierra plainly and matter-of-factly informed me she was taught that "white is right" and that her father was "an Archie Bunker type," ending her narrative with a large, hearty laugh. One could argue that Sierra's laugh was a simple form of discomfort with the narrative, yet, from my perspective, the laugh did not seem awkward, but rather seemed to indicate a pride in her father's bigotry as a lesson that she had learned. As in Pat's case, this is the narrative that Sierra chose to exemplify what she was taught about other groups of people, and thus has the weight of being a socializing experience of import; that is, I did not ask participants to "tell me about a negative lesson you learned about other groups of people." Consequently, that Pat and Sierra shared these stories showed that a negative interaction informed their own color-blind framework.

An aspect of Barbara's narrative indicated Barbara's engagement with naturalization as a causal explanation for the lack of diversity in her mother's friendship circle. When asked about her parents' friends, and whether her parents had predominately white friends or friends from other groups, Barbara attempted to situate herself and her family in expansive language in explaining that her parents' friends where white. Barbara asserted, "Not really, I mean we are not, we are very accepting, and we're not judgmental or discriminatory. It's just that when we lived in Mississippi my mom had a lot of cultural diverse friends and back here not." While Barbara's narrative primarily indicated an abstract liberalism in her establishment of a non-judgmental identity, her relegation of the absence of friends from varied races to geography seemed to display Barbara's belief in the lack of friends as "being just the way it is," or natural. It should be noted that Lilac has a great deal of diversity within the fabric of the community, which can be defined in many ways to many people. I interpret what Barbara said to mean that in "her" Lilac, there was more space for one to choose not to engage in friendships with people other than white people, unlike in Mississippi.

Barbara and her family lived in a nearly exclusively white privileged upper-class self-contained community adjacent to the city of Lilac and full of the resources one might need such as grocery stores, tailors, dry cleaners, banks, restaurants, and so on. Through the descriptions of the other communities where Barbara lived in both South Carolina and in Mississippi, it was clear that, while still privileged, the communities had less racial exclusivity, and more intermingling between white people and Black people was probably an inevitable (naturalization) experience. In a sense, because Barbara has laid out an abstract liberal conceptualization of herself and her family as non-judgmental, the framing of the social circle as absent of people of color in Lilac was a color-blind attempt at a face-saving act (Brown & Levinson, 1987), or in Bonilla-Silva's (2006) language of color-blind rhetoric, Barbara's naturalization narrative had "a positive self-presentation rhetorical goal" (p. 90).

Naturalization is not the most pervasive form of color-blind discourse believed to be used by white people (Bonilla-Silva, 2006), and in this study it was certainly a lesser-included discourse structure used by participants. Still, understanding naturalization is critically important in understanding how color-blind racism operates. The importance of naturalization comes from the idea that "segregation as well as racial preferences are produced through social processes and that is the delusion/illusion" of naturalization as a color-blind approach (p. 56). The naturalization approach is worthy of mention in part because the intentions and consequences of racism often go under-examined. The under-examined nature of race occurs in part because of the belief that ideologies about race are naturally occurring, individualized, and just the way it is, not in fact connected to the larger systemic nature of racism. The testimonies of Barbara, Sierra, and Pat illustrate the power of the socializing effect of naturalization as a form of color-blind discourse.

Minimization

A third discourse strategy of color-blindness is minimization, or use of language positing that while white people "believe discrimination is still a problem, they dispute its salience as a factor explaining Black people's collective standing" (Bonilla-Silva, 2006, p. 43). In minimizing or denying race as a significant factor in people's experiences, white people are able to use rationales to dismiss the importance of race for both white people and non-white people in terms of experience.

Brian was the first participant to engage in a minimization of race. When asked if whiteness shapes the way white teachers teach, Brian responded,

> I don't think so because just because how they grew up and where they grew up was different from where I grew up or *you know* maybe it shaped them, one of my teachers is from Helena, right across the river, and it's more of a city more than anything else; there is no suburbs and if he went to Helena

High that's a big school, big integration and, and most of the minority populated schools around besides the city of Capitol and that might have been
something that shaped him.

Brian's extended narrative deflects away from the question about teachers'
whiteness by minimizing the importance, and then relegates experience to geography, namely, "where they grew up," as being different, without outwardly
saying different from what. In articulating his belief Brian is able to code geography as a proxy for race, but not in a way that enhances the importance of
whiteness as a variable affecting how a white teacher would teach. In fact, Brian
blamed the geography, and if it was "minority populated," then the geography
would be what affects a teacher. Brian's conceptualization places blame on the
minority group while simultaneously using minimization for the effects of
whiteness.

Brian continued with his minimization approach when responding to a
question about students from non-white racial groups needing different instruction from their white peers. Brian responded,

I don't think so! I don't see any reasons why they are any less capable than
anyone and I was actually watching *Law and Order* the other day about affirmative action, but why not just take the name and the race off the application; that way you can't be affirmative action. If they are just seen as equal
they will be taught as equal and when they have problems they will need
help.

Again, using extended narrative, Brian firmly minimized that students of
different races might need a culturally relevant approach to their learning. I find
this minimization interesting, given the general tenor of educational conversations and teachers' over-cited expression that children need differentiated instruction. In denying that non-white students could need and benefit from a culturally relevant experience differentiated to their needs, Brian ignored the
negative effects of racism's history, including how segregated learning experiences, moral inequities, socio-political orientations, and historical underpinnings
have created a debt serviced to children of color in this nation and of which
white children do not bear the cost (Ladson-Billings, 2006b). Brian established
his belief that any experience tailored to the needs of a population of students of
color must be necessitated on the premise that the students are not in fact capable, hence his resistance to engage in what he believed is a more problematic
stance; in essence, Brian had to minimize race if, in his perspective, differentiat-
ing students of color would frame them as deficient, being able to maintain a
positive self-presentation as a rhetorical goal (Bonilla-Silva, 2006).

Finally, Brian would like to minimize the import of affirmative action, articulating that race should just be equal. An interesting caveat is that Brian
wanted not only race removed from the application in his minimization of the
important of race but also he wanted to remove one's name. This orientation

signaled that Brian believed that one's name identifies one's race. In this case, Brian was unable to minimize both, and so the higher order took over; to maintain white interest in employment, race and name should be removed so that everyone has an "equal" shot. By minimizing affirmative action, Brian actually revealed that he did see and judge race not only by what category one checks off on an application, but also in his assumptions of what white and Black names are. Since white women have been the largest beneficiaries of affirmative action in the United States, Brian's response denied a certain historic reality, namely, that it is white people who have most benefited from affirmative action policies. Brian also ignored the historic reality about race that necessitates the continued need for a real affirmative action policy that does not play lip service to minority groups, while simultaneously reifying the white privileging practices that many affirmative action policies have established. In minimizing the importance of affirmative action, Brian also was able to minimize the over five hundred year history of racial inequity in the United States that necessitates affirmative action and policies such as Title VII. Brian is not alone, as five of the United States Supreme Court justices in the previously discussed *Ricci et al. v. DeSteffano et al.* case share Brian's outlook.

Like Brian, Barbara engaged in minimization as a color-blind discourse strategy. When asked if students from under-represented groups need different instruction from their white peers, Barbara claimed, "I don't think so. I think everybody is equal and as long as you instill that's your point." Her minimization is interesting; while she articulated a similar, equal treatment argument as Brian, Barbara articulated some belief that the minimization has to be socialized as "that's your point" when working with others. This equality tension that arises with minimization is interesting. If equal treatment was the goal and I owned a shoe factory, I would give everybody the same size shoe, or equal treatment. If I were to be equitable as the shoe factory owner, I would find out the needs of those who require shoes and create a complement of shoes in various sizes that fit the wearer. The ideal that race should be minimized in the name of equal treatment misses the point that students being treated equally is likely to replicate inequity and exacerbate an already problematic and segregated schooling experience that many of the nation's children of color receive.

Color-Blindness and Incoherence

I draw from Sierra to transition between minimization as a rhetorical strategy of color-blindness and the confusing and incoherent narratives exhibited by participants. Sierra's narrative was, in part, centered on minimization and clearly was an incoherent narrative. When Sierra was asked if her white teachers' teaching styles changed with respect to teaching children from different racial background Sierra pointed to a very specific example:

> Uhm, my French teacher was harsh to the Black kid in our class but it wasn't
> just because he was Black, he just sat there and he was engaged and would
> learn and stuff but she just, her idea of a good student was one that was quiet
> and sat there and did work.

Initially Sierra attempted to minimize the attribution of her teacher's behavior as being racially linked. Sierra, however, only partially minimized, asserting that "it wasn't just because he was Black." In her statement, Sierra identified that the harsh treatment received was if not fully, at least particularly, because he was Black. Further, what was it that the teacher was seeking, beyond the student's race, that he allegedly did not provide that would warrant the treatment he received? Sierra said that "he just sat there and he was engaged and would learn." To me as a former classroom teacher and teacher educator, the student described appears to be angelic and ideal, a student who apparently has self-control to sit in class, to be engaged, and to learn, a simulacrum that seems to have never existed within student populations. Sierra tried to justify and minimize the harsh treatment the student received as not being linked to race by explaining that the student was not the teacher's "idea of a good student." Based on Sierra's description of the student, the student's behavior, and what the teacher looked for in a student, the only element that seems to be non-concordant is the student's race. So in attempting to minimize the importance of race, Sierra's narrative became confused and confusing and appeared to not sustain a minimizing approach to color-blindness.

Sierra's lack of coherence when talking about race was not unique. In fact, Bob, Pat, Sierra, Angela, Steven, and Cathy all exhibited a fair level of incoherence when speaking generally about race. In chapter 7, I will also present how the incoherence moved beyond general discussions of race and presented itself specifically when speaking of identity. In this chapter, however, I will limit the presentation narrative incoherence solely to general discussion of the topic of race.

When asked if students from underrepresented groups needed instruction different from white peers, Bob responded,

> Like the teacher I'm with now is always on the projector doing like number
> one this is how you do it, number two, and you OK it's just example after
> example and they are not learning anything whereas they just need to get
> more engaged in what they are doing but ehh I don't uhm jeez what was the
> question again?

In part, Bob presented what appeared to be pedagogy that was not engaging in itself; the responsibility for engagement was placed back on students as exhibited in his assertion "they just need to get more engaged," as if students have the control over how material is presented and can make the experience more engaging. Bob avoided direct discussion of race and direct response to the question asked; he began to lose track and became very incoherent as evidenced by his statement "but ehh I don't uhm jeez what was the question again?" When the question was reworded specifically as, "Do Black or Latino students, for example, need different types of instruction from white peers?" Bob's response was no less coherent when he said,

> Ohh yeah. No. Just more patience with inner-city school and all kids are capable of doing the same thing just because they are Black white Asian or whatever means they always learn but one way is best for them but it's not gonna change just because you are a different color and the kids that are more fiscally sound I guarantee you that all the Caucasian kids are mixed and matched for learning style and you just have to figure out, I'm not gonna teach them any different.

Bob's extended, complex narrative was also rather incoherent as he tried to cover several bases in defending whiteness through the use of a color-blind approach. The question asked on the follow-up was racially specific and left less room for ambiguity than asking about marginalized groups in general. Bob was initially confused with the general question of marginalized groups; when asked very specifically about race, he employed racial deflection and shifted the response to say that inner-city schoolchildren need patience, relegating issues of race back to geographic location, and intimating that Black and Latino students do not exist in suburban or rural settings.

Bob moved to establish the abstractly liberal idea that "all kids are capable of doing the same thing" yet added a layer of confusion and racial ambiguity when he asserted "just because they are Black, white, Asian or whatever." In his conceptualization, Latino groups, one of the groups specifically referenced in the question, are removed, Asian groups inserted, and a new racial class of "whatever" is created. Bob also totalized the discourse in his use of the word "just," as if the question asked whether students from under-represented groups receive different instruction solely because of, or to use Bob's language, "just" due to race; clearly that was not what the question asked.

Bob's combining of concepts was confusing; he totalized the question to race being the whole and only essence of a student, and then deflected by stringing together a rapid-fire set of racial groups. Bob ended his narrative with a discussion of students being "fiscally sound; white students were attended to by being "mixed and matched for learning style," and he ended saying that he has to "figure out" what students need despite the fact that he is simultaneously "not gonna teach them any different." In the entire confused narrative, many concepts were brought to bear, and the question posed went mostly unanswered.

Pat's narrative about race also was incoherent and confusing. When asked about the racial or ethnic makeup of her and her family's friendship circle, Pat responded, "It's like my dad had a lot of friends and still does but my mom, whenever she gets close to someone they always end up passing away and so she kind of likes just to have associates I guess from work, but she's getting a little bit more." First and foremost, Pat's narrative response did not answer the question presented and Pat danced past race and ethnicity to just talk generally about her parents' friends or lack thereof, that is, her dad's having "a lot of friends" and her mother's fear of friendship due to the fact that "they always end up passing away."

Pat's confusing and incoherent narratives did not end with her family's friendship circle. When asked if students who were not white were treated or taught differently by teachers, Pat said,

> That's hard because it's different perspective. Remembering now I wouldn't say so but we didn't have that many so I think maybe there was some pre-conceived notions. There would be if there was a conflict, teachers would just assume certain things and so I am sure it happened but I didn't personally pay attention to that.

Like Bob, Pat took on simultaneously conflicting positions that added to the confusion of the narrative. First Pat stated that "it's different perspective," and after looking over her transcript several times and listening to her interview, I am still unsure what different perspective it is that she was referencing. Pat went on to say that differing treatment did not happen, but said that the reason was that there were not "that many"; I interpret Pat's "that many" statement to mean not "that many" students from non-white backgrounds. In the same statement, however, Pat said, "I think there were some pre-conceived notions," which appears to contradict her idea that teachers did not treat students differently.

The narrative became more confusing when Pat said that "if there was a conflict," the "teachers would just assume certain things," and she ended with a 180-degree switch of position, claiming that she was "sure it happened." Then she absolved herself from any negative implications in the assertion that she "didn't personally pay attention." In her attempt to respond to the question from many color-blind angles, Pat contradicted her own statements, all the while presenting a confusing and fairly incoherent narrative.

I asked Pat about where she wanted to teach and received perhaps the longest extended response in the entire set of interviews among participants. Pat did not use overtly racial language, but used geography and other codes as proxies for race:

> I am very open to it now and I don't want to make that decision but I thought about maybe teaching in the city school district because I want that challenge and they have that bad reputation of needing so much help and I want to have impact but if you are a good teacher you can be a good teacher anywhere and I haven't really made that choice and I haven't had that experience, and maybe I will realize that I'm not capable of doing this and so I just know I don't want to be in a rural because it is too far from where I am from and so possibly the more common urban areas. I would like to leave the state, I would. North Carolina, because I have always wanted to go down

there and I think it is a great area and there especially now I have that chance to travel to places bigger than Lilac and I want to teach in the South because I want to have that Northeastern impact because the Northeast is known for their high standards and their high requirements and take that and put that somewhere to raise their standards but I couldn't do the Deep South because I would be frustrated with their standards for the students because I hold myself even higher than northeastern, don't be mediocre and I feel like they don't even have those standards and they would be really low and I would expect too much of them and that lifestyle down there too I can't eat seafood either so I don't know that would probably be a damper on my living situation but like maybe I'll miss home and want to come back and Teach For America is another thing I want to do for experiences because they put you in the roughest of areas and those kids really need help and if I'm young and if you want experience you jump right in there and I may cry every day but at the end I will be a much stronger teacher.

Pat presented a significantly extended narrative that switched from topic to topic with little organization or coherence and seemingly was stated in one breath. Pat did reveal some significant aspects of her racialized beliefs in the narrative, again through the proxy of geography. Pat conceptualized the experience of teaching in city schools as challenging: the South, particularly "down South," supposedly lacks standards for education, and the roughest areas are allegedly a good model for professional development and on-site learning of what it means to be a teacher. Ladson-Billings (2006b) has argued that the nation's children of color are suffering from the effects of an educational debt lodged against them, and for teachers, seeking the training of "hard knocks" from teaching in areas most affected by the debt seems an ill-fated move that is unlikely to help children of color in any significant way. So even if Pat were to learn from those experiences to be a better teacher, it would come at the expense of the children and families most affected by the racist orientations of Jim Crow segregation that provided the foundation for our modern education system. The narrative shows, furthermore, that Pat has an extremely confused, incoherent, and cursory understanding of the reality for the places and spaces she references in the narrative.

Sierra was asked if teachers' whiteness shapes the way they taught her. Sierra presented a short but confusing narrative, responding, "It's hard to say because they didn't have a diverse student population but I would have to say yes because I don't know." In Sierra's response we see a fundamental belief that whiteness matters only in contexts where students are not white. I argue now, and will argue later when directly addressing White Racial Identity in chapter 7, that a teacher's whiteness is more salient and significant in a setting when teaching an all, or predominately, white student population. Opportunities abound to socialize with white students about what it means to be white, for white racial bonding, and to share the nature of the segregated experience of being only with white people. Sierra interprets whiteness as being influential only when the white teachers teach students who are not white, which is ultimately a defensive position about one's racial identity as opposed to the recognition of whiteness' presence in every white person's set of experiences. The confusion and incoherence in Sierra's narrative came from the tenets of her belief system when she asserted, "But I would have to say yes because I don't know." If she did not know, Sierra simply could have articulated that she did not know, but she felt compelled to argue the affirmative despite not knowing and, in doing so, complicated and confused the utterance, making this narrative incoherent.

Angela also articulated a level of incoherence in her narrative about race by deflecting her response from the posed question. When asked if students from under-represented groups need different types of instruction from their white peers, Angela presented this incoherent narrative: "I have always thought about kids that learn visually should be taught *you know* make sure you have every learning style but I have never thought about how race could play into that." Angela did not approximate an answer to the specifics of the question and likened the question to an abstract discussion of learning style, asserting at the end that she had not thought about "it," unwilling to use the word "race" directly. I was confused by her response and unable to understand what she said, beyond likening race to learning style and learning style being her primary consideration.

When asked if students in his schools were diverse, Steven's position was confusing and somewhat incoherent. Steven said, "Yeah I had different views of some of them. Why are they even here they are not even doing anything? They just get in trouble all the time." Fundamentally, the question asked Steven if there was diversity in the student population, yet Steven saw the question as an opening to present his own opinion on "diverse" students' very existence in the landscape of the school; he questioned if they should even attend since, from his perspective, they did not do anything and just got in trouble all the time. Steven seemed to communicate in this narrative that kids who do not meet a standard of what he believes to be "doing something" simply should not come to school anymore. Ironically, his narrative glossed over an important consideration that diverse student populations are often considered to be school dependent, do in fact come to school, most often have excellent attendance, and try to engage with a schooling system that simply refuses to engage them. The entire schooling experience becomes a catch-22 for students: when they go to school, teachers wonder, "Why are you here?" and when they do not come to school, teachers create a narrative of "Those people – they are lazy and just don't value education." Steven's narrative was confusing and incoherent to the extent that he never really answered the question in depth but, rather, used the space of the question as a sounding board; his suggestion seemed not only implausible but did not make sense for someone who is one semester away from having his own classroom and serving the public in the role of teacher.

Cathy's confusing and incoherent narrative was perhaps the single most illustrative example of incoherence and deflection from a direct question about race. When asked if she ever had teachers from races other than white, Cathy responded,

> Yes, I had a lot of different teachers (seven second pause), let me think here, uhm (eight second pause). I have had teachers that are very liberal from one side or the other and try to push their opinions on you which I don't really agree with, I have also had teachers come from different backgrounds like the straight-A student that wasn't popular and went to college to the kid that did bad in high school but then went to the Marines and got a good education and so their perspectives in teaching are different.

Cathy's response was extremely incoherent; she clearly did not address race, and even with extra extended pausing, was able to engage only with circumlocutions that approximated the subject of the question; she never addressed the foundation of the question of whether she had teachers other than white teachers.

Whiteness as Property and Semantic Moves

In all of its forms, from abstract liberalism marked by its expansive engagement of being non-judgmental coupled with highly judgmental language, to naturalization, to minimization, and finally to incoherence, the semantic moves of color-blind discourse give participants extra room to move around and through discussions of race. Creating rhetorical space, color-blind language permits participants an avenue to avoid taking positions by ignoring and denying, or by presenting incoherence; when taking positions, the couched beliefs of this study's participants might have been perceived as racist, with open ideological language of acceptance and being free of judgment. Regardless of the particular type of color-blind approach, the semantic moves were deployed by participants when the nature of the questions involved race, a finding consistent with Bonilla-Silva's (2001, 2006) research that the occurrence of the semantic moves of color-blind discourse most often appear as the nature of the questions has increasingly racialized language, racialized perspective, or even perceived racialized perspective on the part of participants.

In considering the meaning of both white racial bonding and color-blind discourse, I revert to the literature in Critical Race Theory (CRT), and particularly the concept of whiteness as property. Whiteness as property suggests that whiteness, an absolute with a certain level of inalienability, carries values to those who possess it (Harris, 1995). For white people, the high sense of value attached to whiteness promotes whiteness' property function. A key idea behind property value becomes how white people negotiate the maintenance of said value particularly, since to possess whiteness is also to have an absolute and inherent goodness (DeCuir-Gunby, 2006).

Harris (1995) asserts that white people capitalize on whiteness for the purposes of socializing and enjoyment and, as such, bonding amongst white people helps white people to solidify and share in the high value placed on the reputation of whiteness. One of the functions of whiteness' property value is its "absolute right to exclude" (Harris, 1995, p. 282). Typically, whiteness is defined not by its characteristics, which would force whiteness to become a stable entity easily identified and consequently addressed, but rather by what it is not; as such, white people are able to exclude those "deemed not to be white" (Harris, 1995, p. 283).

In this study, the deployment of semantic moves, such as white racial bonding and the use of color-blind orientations to express racialized beliefs, is suggestive of the need white people have to maintain the value of their whiteness. The semantic moves become a defensive posture by which the core value of whiteness can be defended. In particular, white people draw from "stock stories" (Delgado, 1993), which serve as a type of master narrative that socializes white people to the meaning of white people and is used as ammunition in the deployment of semantic moves targeted to protect whiteness' property value. Without being challenged or having it brought to their attention, it is likely that these teachers would not admit or acknowledge the role of color-blind racism or white racial bonding, as calling attention to such approaches necessarily opens the opportunity for whiteness' value to be weakened.

I refer to Harris' (1995) descriptions of the characteristics of whiteness as property in thinking specifically about how both the semantic moves presented in these findings are indicative of the maintenance of whiteness property value. All four characteristics highlight how whiteness is understood and show how it is maintained as possessing property value:

> *Disposition*: whiteness confers rewards based on certain behaviors of whiteness
>
> *Use and enjoyments*: whiteness, having certain privileges, is enjoyable for those who possess it as they can benefit in the privileges
>
> *Reputation and status*: given the nature of the benefits and privileges of whiteness, whiteness necessarily has a reputation and status that need to be maintained, which leads directly into
>
> *An absolute right to exclude:* because of the rewards, use and enjoyments, and reputation of whiteness, white people use an absolute right to exclude in order to maintain the previous three elements.

The participants' semantic moves demonstrated all four conditions of whiteness as property value. First, participants' use of white racial bonding and color-blind discourse helped to establish, through affinity, particular types of behaviors consistent across the narratives. By consistently engaging in the same semantic moves, the study's participants established the nature of disposition, that is, they understood the behaviors of whiteness that confer rewards and benefits. Further, participants used discourse in modeling the coherent behaviors of whiteness and attempted to confirm shared meaning of those dispositions through the bonding move of "you know.

The second evident characteristic is the use and enjoyment of whiteness. In the denial that occurred through color-blind orientations when discussing racial others, participants deflected from beliefs which might frame their whiteness as bad or questionable. If their whiteness was bad, overt and covert, privileges would not be possible. In establishing color-blind discourse, participants created distance from irrational white people who have jeopardized the enjoyment of whiteness through their racism. From the participants' perspectives, white overt racists threaten how enjoyable whiteness can be, so there is a great necessity to distance oneself from any orientation that appears racist in nature; the use and enjoyment of whiteness can then be received without one's being responsible for the negative aspects of racism. Ironically, the white racial bonding demonstrated the participants' willingness to share in the nature of whiteness and establish beliefs in the comfort of being with another white; thus, whatever they said could protect their whiteness from outside threats, as long as they could establish a shared meaning and affinity through bonding. In part, this is why I argue that had a researcher of color engaged the same participants, the nature of protecting the use and enjoyment of whiteness would have necessitated an abandonment of white racial bonding; this shift would have increased hyper-color-blind orientations and different semantic moves that demonstrated to the non-white researcher that the participant was a good white and thus would not threaten the participants' sense of white privilege.

The third consideration is the reputation and status of whiteness. As a type of semantic move, color-blind orientations are particularly apt to help maintain the reputation and status of whiteness. As has been suggested, color-blind orientations create rhetorical distance from racism and the other ills of white people that do not shed positively on the reputation and status of whiteness. White people do not want to create a situation where whiteness can be damaged, and thus use their rhetoric to attempt to shield themselves from responsibility for problematic beliefs, and consequently, are able to maintain a positive reputation and status of their whiteness.

Finally, whiteness as property value has the absolute right to exclude. The white racial bonding that occurred in this study as semantic moves to discuss race have been presented thus far for what they do to connect white people to fellow white people. As with any concept, I suggest that the anti-concept is also necessary to fully understanding what is in place. Whereas the bonding is inclusive of white people, the bonding is anti- or non-inclusive of those who are not white. Conversely, had the researcher in this study been a faculty member of color, the racial bonding semantic move would have been absent. In bonding and claiming affinity, the white participant not only bonds with the white researcher in this case, but she or he establishes that anyone who is not white will not be included in the bond but rather excluded from the inner workings of whiteness; thus the absolute right to exclude is obtained.

If we understand property as an intellectual material, as Ladson-Billings and Tate (1995) have suggested, teachers' decisions about how to approach their craft will inherently privilege the property and property value that they hold. Consequently, there exists a possessive investment and interest in whiteness to protect the nature of the intellectual materials that form how white people, and in this case white teachers, see the world. Thus the conversation about how semantic moves are demonstrative of whiteness property value is far more than a theoretical conversation. In understanding how the semantic moves used by participants represent the whiteness property value, we also have a window into the way in which white people use their privileged position to shape their epistemological standpoint and understandings of others. The view of self and others directly affects how white teachers shape their craft and how they value students who either possess or do not possess their similar property value expressed in race. As we will see in chapter 7, this view influences the construction of one's racial identity.

Chapter 5
Naïveté in Rationales for Being Teachers

One of the greatest challenges in twenty-first century urban education is the re-cruitment and retention of highly qualified, effective, committed teachers who have well- developed rationales for entering the field. Throughout my profes-sional career, I have witnessed the consequences to K–12 students when their teachers are able to generate only generic commitments to teaching and conse-quently possess under-developed rationales for doing the work. When the teach-er has not thought about the *why* of the work in a meaningful way, she or he is likely to wander through the enterprise of education without deriving specific approaches to her or his craft that are consistent with why she or he does the work. That is to say, if my rationale for teaching is to prepare the democratic citizenry of the next generation, ideas of citizenship and democracy would per-meate every aspect of my teaching; the teaching that occurs is for and with stu-dents, as opposed to being oriented by primarily content-driven considerations. In my own teaching, as when I worked with students on how to write letters in fourth grade, I had my students research a meaningful problem in our communi-ty, and we wrote letters to the elected leaders who could help to effect change. A teacher with a naïve or under-developed rationale is likely to teach letter writing to students as opposed to teaching students to write a letter, and she or he is also likely to orient the experience of writing the letter in decontextualized ways, such as writing to an imaginary friend. In such decontextualized learning situa-tions, students are not meaningfully involved in an active and engaged set of experiences. While I am not suggesting that all teachers develop citizenship as their rationale, I am suggesting that having a developed, coherent, and informed rationale for doing the work of teaching can serve to help drive the instruction in meaningful ways. Unfortunately in education, we hear teachers often say, "I am teaching math" or "I am teaching *Romeo and Juliet*," as if inanimate things can be taught. We rarely hear student-first language in the teaching enterprise.

The pre-service teacher participants in my research by and large did not articulate well-developed or complex rationales for their desire to be teachers. In

fact, their rationales could be understood both as naïve and perhaps another semantic move around race. The pervasive and overwhelming number of white
teachers, and the staggering statistics that children of color are most likely to be
taught by white teachers in mostly (re)segregated schooling environments,
makes the discussion of teacher rationale important from not merely an employment and training perspective but also from a racial perspective. The struggle to break from the historic, moral, socio-political, and economic debts (Ladson-Billings, 2006b) that have dominated the framing of current educational
opportunities in school systems is particularly complicated given the importance
of the intended role of teacher as an agent of change and socialization. Schools
need teachers who are not only competently and thoughtfully prepared to teach
but who are also clear about why it is that they are doing the work and are sure
of the implication that the teacher's own race has on the educational opportunities and socialization that children receive.

I will argue in chapter 6 that the teacher's racial identity is important not
just when the identity may differ from that of her or his students. Given the socializing powers teachers have, a thoughtful understanding of why one wants to
be a teacher and the power of a teacher's race are important in the socialization
of any child from any racial background, a precursor to the discussion of racial
identity later in this book. There appear to be high levels of apathy among
teachers; new teachers, particularly in high-needs districts, are unlikely to be
retained through three years of teaching.

The naïve rationales presented in this chapter suggest that the participants in
this study were unable to articulate rationales for becoming a teacher that would
help them enter the profession ready and prepared for the challenges of educating in the twenty-first century. Moreover, the articulation of naïve perspectives
seems to serve as another semantic move that demonstrates the color-blindness
of white pre-service teachers and seems to block an engagement with culturally
relevant pedagogies.

During the first interview, participants were asked directly about their reasons and rationales for becoming teachers. While there was much variety in
terms of the participants' responses, the data suggests that many of their positions were not well informed or, at best, lacked complex development. Brian, for
example, could state only that he had wanted to be a teacher since he was in
ninth grade but gave no specific rationale about why, stating, "When I was in
ninth grade, I knew I wanted to be a teacher, and I don't know why or what
drew me." Brian went on to say that he had a teacher he thought was "the cool-
est guy," and "I always knew that I kind of wanted to coach and he was a coach
. . . there were engaging teachers and coaches and I was just like, I think I can do
that." Brian went on to articulate a cliché about being a teacher, stating, "It's just
that I care what happens to kids," followed by, "If you want to be an astronaut,
sure, I'll write you a reference letter." Brian's lighthearted approach to talking
about the profession was reflected in the comment that really caring would include writing a reference for the position of astronaut. In his narrative, Brian did

not demonstrate an ability to work through the realities of the lives of his students who are unlikely to be astronauts; rather, he presented a generic and color-blind narrative to support his rationale to be a teacher.

Like Brian, Barbara did not articulate a rationale that appeared to have depth. Barbara shared that co-workers and fellow students suggested that she become a teacher. In particular, Barbara stated, "A co-worker was like, you love history; why not go to school for education, and when I had that epiphany moment with her, I know I was going about it all wrong." The so-called epiphany moment was really not related to the profession itself but more to the fact that she liked history, and education would create the ability to have gainful employment relative to her interests and likes. Barbara also shared that she did not "want to work in a restaurant [her] entire life." Barbara switched majors from hospitality to education and ultimately said, "Teaching is something I always wanted to do." In her responses, Barbara shared that a love of content brought her to the profession but she did not speak specifically about what a teacher does, how teachers connect with children, develop curriculum, or anything else that would give insight into her career choice. When asked what she would like students to know about her choice to become a teacher, Barbara stated,

> I want to help and being a teacher is a good way to do that. I want to be that positive role model because I never got in trouble and I'm not the bad kid so to speak and I always told myself at a young age that I wasn't afraid to do anything, whatever, I don't know that could make me very naïve or the greatest person on earth.

Barbara articulated the cliché of educator as helper, then redirected the conversation from the act of teacher and back toward herself and her own experience as never getting in trouble or being "the bad kid." Barbara's responses appear to indicate that either she had not thought through the more serious implications of the profession, or she had not developed a discourse to be able to articulate her true understandings of the profession.

Bob also did not articulate a rationale for teaching that delved beyond either the surface or the clichés about the teaching profession that dominate the wider parlance about teachers and education. In particular, Bob related his choice to becoming a teacher back to his father's work situation, stating, "You see that and, you, I don't want that. I want to go to college and better myself, getting a high-paying job so that I don't have to do that kind of work." The desire to better his perceived lot in life is admirable but does not necessarily explain that teaching alone would accomplish this goal, particularly since teachers make low salaries relative to other careers for which Bob could study as an undergraduate. When asked specifically about why he was choosing a career in education, Bob began to articulate cliché and surface-level reasons, stating,

Since middle school I knew I wanted to be a teacher and making a difference in kids' lives. I loved the idea of guiding kids or something like that.
I know that I want to do sports and I have always been good at sports and I
just love it and it's relaxing to me at the same time math came easy to me.

Bob went on to share that he looked to be either a physical education teacher or
a math teacher, and that he knew he "wanted to have summers off and be a phys.
ed. teacher because that's just the easiest job teaching ever you just play sports
all day." Righteous College did not offer a teacher preparation program in physical education, so Bob decided that he "always liked math" and would pursue
that major at Righteous.

With vagueness, Angela also discussed her perceptions about her choice to
be a teacher. When asked about her decision to become a teacher and an education major, Angela stated, "I love social studies and I love politics and history,
and it's always been interesting to me and I could talk about politics, and social
studies and history until I am blue in the face and so I think I should teach." Angela also stated that she was influenced by two teachers whoshe felt developed
her interest in history, and that for students, she wants to "make them care." Angela was not specific about what making students care meant, or how as a teacher her role would allow her to develop an ethos of care among her potential future students. Angela stated that one should "want to teach" to be a teacher,
citing a generic phrase often used by education majors to explain the desire to
teach; Angela went on to state, "I really try to make myself one of the teachers I
feel is there because they want to be there." While this sentiment is positive in
nature it does not explain beyond a surface level why she wants to teach or the
conditions that would demonstrate she has met the goal of wanting to be there.

Todd also displayed a rationale for teaching that appeared to be vague and
under-developed. Todd stated, "Not to toot my own horn, but they [referring to
his family] always say I would be a good teacher because I'm not shy in front of
people and have no problem like I'll get up and talk in front of anyone." Todd is
right that being a teacher does require that he talk in front of people, but this
rationale provided to him by his family does not robustly account for the complexities of the profession beyond a technical aspect of talking to groups of people. Certainly the public speaking dimension of teaching is also not unique to the
profession and would be a requisite for many fields of study, so it provides no
particular explanation of the choice to be a teacher.

Todd did explain that he sees the role of teaching as being unique, asserting
that "from a legal standpoint my job is to teach them that curriculum, but more
than that my job is to connect with them and help them." Todd uses a reductionist approach as he describes a main "legal" purpose of his work as content delivery. Content delivery is but one aspect of teaching and, ultimately, if the prospective teacher sees content delivery as the major purpose of her or his job, the
conceptualization of teacher is reduced to that of information specialist. The
reductionist vision of self as teacher, coupled with a vague and cliché notion of

teachers as helpers, does not sustain an in-depth understanding of the reason to be a teacher. Todd continued with cliché in his assertion that "choosing to become a teacher is me taking an oath to do my best to help them." Todd is unable to move beyond teacher as helper and teacher as a technician delivering content to explain why it is that he wants to be a teacher or how being a teacher will do the "helping" that he proposes for kids.

Cathy also articulated a very confused position about why she wants to be a teacher. In part, Cathy said that being a teacher comes from having good models of teachers, but it is her explanation of what her models are that gives one pause. Cathy said that teachers "influenced me, especially the diverse teachers that I had, how I could have one history teacher that was an ex-Marine but he taught just as well as any teachers maybe of a different race. I thought it was cool that so many races and religions could still be good teachers and it didn't matter. (Pause) It doesn't matter?" Cathy asserted that race does not matter, then paused for a long second, and turned her statement into a question, as though seeking my approval to assure her that race did not, in fact, matter. It is interesting that, in her conceptualization of teacher, Cathy placed emphasis on aspects such as military service and was surprised that either service or race could create a situation for the teacher to also be good. Cathy's position that this was the model that motivated her to pursue teaching is confusing analytically, as she did not really provide what it is about those teachers that served as a model for her, beyond hypothetical and undefined race and military service.

In attempting to further explain how she arrived at becoming a teacher, Cathy bounced from topic to topic, never providing a response that would illuminate her understanding of the profession she chose. When asked why she wanted to major in education and be a teacher, Cathy's extended response was:

> I have always loved history and knew I wanted to do something with history; my dad and uncle were history majors, it runs in our families. Also I do like to help people, and I do like teaching, and my sister will be, like, help me with this and I like having the work to help her get to know it and it makes me happy. I have always taught sports camps and my uncle was principal of our middle school.

In this response, Cathy jumped from her love of history, to family love of history, to helping her sister, to teaching sports camps, to having a family member as a principal. Having family members in education, Cathy had the potential to be able to make deeper connections to the profession, and even potentially to have a language to explain why teaching makes sense. Like other participants, though, ultimately Cathy came back to the idea of teacher as helper and displayed a sort of interest convergence between her personal interests and choice of content. When asked to discuss what she wanted students to know about her choice to be a teacher, Cathy ended with, "I am very serious about the fact that I really do like history and how it helps later in life and all that." The over-focus on content, particularly her personal affection for the content, coupled with a lack of discussion about the students in meaningful ways, seems disconnected from an understanding of teacher beyond the surface.

Steven also was unable to articulate substantive reasons why teaching was his chosen profession. When asked why he wanted to be a teacher, Steven articulated, "I thought, I'm gonna be a teacher; it's like so easy," an articulation similar to Bob's thinking. Further Steven saw his role as twofold, helping to "educate *them* [students] on information that they are gonna need to know for the test but also build relationships with them"; he further stated his wish was for students to go home and say, "Mr. Paper did this with me today and it was so much fun." Steven's desire for students to have fun does not appear to be a substantive approach to teaching in and of itself. The concept of teacher as test preparer becomes, in a way, a reification of an autocratic teacher as technician who must focus on test results as a measure of teacher efficacy. In essence, Steven as test-preparer espouses a self-regulated view of teaching that aligns with the lay discourse on what teachers' roles are, yet falls short of being a clear vision of what teacher education hopes to prepare teachers to be.

Sierra had been around the "majors" circuit in her time as an undergraduate; as the oldest participant in the study, she has been working continuously on her undergraduate degree for the better part of seven years and has majored in many fields. After her penultimate major of photography did not pan out, Sierra asserted, "I started thinking about my backup plan to become a French teacher; my grandmother is Canadian French and that was my backup plan so I was like, OK, I want to go into teaching; I want to be a teacher." Sierra's only real other discussion about why she wanted to be a teacher came when asked what she would want students to know about her choice of profession; like previous participants, Sierra centered on the role of her content, saying, "I teach them because (six second pause) I love my subject and I want them to learn it too and that I am there to be a role model." Sierra's response echoed many of the participants who balanced both their personal interest in the subject with the formula response of teacher as helper and role model.

Of all the participants, Pat shared what appeared to be the most in-depth and substantive ideas of why she wanted to be a teacher and her rationale for choosing the field. Pat cited that being a social studies teacher is important in order to help students "become better citizens." The response shows some thinking that matches the aims of being a social studies teacher and the goal of a free public education to promote democratic ideals of citizenship consistent with the National Council for the Social Studies' standards. Pat was ultimately unable to describe how her role as a teacher would serve in pursuit of the development of the citizenry and future electorate, however, and consequently while her articulation was positive, it remained at the surface.

Pat also believed that planning lessons, an important aspect of a teacher's professional obligation, is wasteful and not a productive organizational tool for her as a teacher; she said, "It's just not how I like to be organized," and said her mentor shared that she would need lesson plans only as pacification of administrators. Her mentor is alleged to have told her, "When you get into a school your superintendent wants this BS kind of stuff." Pat also shared that being "real" is an important concern for her; she stated that she learned from her mentor about having students see her as "human," stating, "I don't want students mad at me," a negative perception of teachers she thinks are "disciplinarian[s]." Pat's responses indicated that despite wanting students to "become better," she is not particularly interested in planning or management as a part of that pursuit, nor did she develop how a teacher engages her students in the act of developing the ideals of citizenry.

Discussion

The gaps between white and non-white students can be understood as being exacerbated by any number of factors that loosely fall into the categories of educational debt that Ladson-Billings (2006b) has pointed out have shaped the landscape of American education since the beginning of so-called "free" and public schools. The challenges of teaching in the twenty-first century are not limited to the act of teaching and delivering instruction; the gaps that exist between students are microcosms of the larger gap in wealth, material worth, employment opportunities, and livelihood between whites and non-white peers across age spans throughout the nation and the world. The school then can be understood as a site where the gaps that persist into adulthood are formed—the basin of inequity.

In this discussion then, the role of the teacher cannot be limited to stereotypic constructions of what a teacher is, if the challenge of paying off the debt is to be addressed. As presented in chapter 1, it is very difficult to retain teachers in high-needs districts, and there is a phenomenon of white flight, whereby new, white teachers rapidly leave the profession. Teacher education can only do so to prepare teachers for their roles. Teacher candidates, and even many teacher educators, reduce instructional opportunities to issues of methods and approaches to delivering instruction, leaving the question and discussion of their identity, and particularly racial identity, unspoken. In an approach with either too much focus on methods to the exclusion of broader perspective, or too much focus on sweepingly broad claims about the aims of education without meaningful mechanisms for reaching said goals, a crucial aspect of race is left unsaid and remains color-blind (Bonilla-Silva, 2006). When the racial identity of the teacher is left unexamined, and the teacher is unable to see her or his work as a teacher as being that of a political agent of change with a developed and substantive rationale, the ability for the teacher to situate the work within a culturally relevant approach is lost.

The generic and naïve ways in which the pre-service teachers articulated their desires to be teachers demonstrates a certain abstract color-blindness insofar as a seemingly expansive narrative is deployed but a restrictive approach is engaged. I am asserting that these methods-based and "I want to help kids" orientations articulated by pre-service teachers are naïve in their nature and help pre-service teachers maintain a blindness to the ways in which the teachers' identities, including their white racial identities, affect their interactions as a socializing force for students. Ultimately, not developing one's rationale while in the pre-service teacher education phase works to support the long-standing hegemonic system that has privileged white people and has kept peoples of color at the margins (hooks, 2003). Further, in a dysconscious way, the unexamined, naïve, and under-developed rationales for becoming a teacher prevent pre-service teachers from engaging in the selective and intentional use of approaches that complement the reality of the particular classroom settings of which the teacher is a part in a meaningful and culturally relevant manner (Dixson & Fasching-Varner, 2008). Consequently, understanding that pre-service teachers do not possess sufficiently developed rationales for becoming educators becomes significant not only in what it tells us about the pre-service teacher's choice to become a teacher, but also with respect to the way that naïve rationales become another set of semantic moves whereby one's race and the implications of race go unspoken; the work becomes racially dysconscious or subconscious. When new teachers enter the classroom racially dysconscious or subconscious, they may attempt to employ methods that were taught to them in their pre-service teacher education programs, using hypothetical children and without consideration for the socio-emotive and socio-political realities of the classroom landscape they are in in particular, or, more pointedly, the socio-political realities of the students' lives. Instead of learning the thinking behind the intended engagement of a particular method or strategy, the teacher clings to the method itself, decontextualized from who the students are (as raced, gendered, sexualized, classed, abled, etc.), who he or she is as teacher (as raced, gendered, sexualized, classed, abled, etc.), and the resulting pedagogy becomes as naïve as the rationales the teachers have for becoming teachers, or what has been suggested as "free and reduced pedagogy" (Fasching-Varner & Dodo Seriki, 2012).

Upon entering the profession, new teachers often find that "methods" learned in their pre-service teacher education programs are ineffective at reaching the particular population of students in their classrooms. The new teachers may become upset at the method's apparent inefficacy. Once upset by a method's perceived inefficacy, new teachers are apt to dismiss their pre-service teacher education as too idealistic and/or blame the students, attributing the lack of efficacy to "problems" with the students, often a code for what they believe are deficiencies attributed to race, home life, socio-economic status, parenting, and so on.

New teachers are often apt to characterize the children as the "reality" that prevents them from engaging their students instructionally, and teachers often become defensive about a culturally relevant praxis, citing that the "reality" is less idealistic than they were taught. Eventually, when new teachers have exhausted all the largely ineffective methods or "tricks of the trade" learned in their teacher education program, they become frustrated with the job. I believe it is in the moment of frustration with their job that the finding of this study takes on its secondary meaning. When frustrated within their jobs early in their career, young teachers are likely to contemplate a question such as, "Why am I even doing this at all?" In asking the question and thinking about their rationale for being a teacher, they are left with what participants in this study came up with: "I like kids"; "I want to help"; "I thought it was gonna be easy"; "I wanted summers off"; "I really like the subject matter"; what emerges is that there is not a substantial or substantive reason to stay, and their uninformed identity, marked by the semantic move of naïveté, creates the urge to leave the classroom.

The semantic moves they employ that are color-blind in nature (from chapter 4) combined with the lack of rationale for doing the work do not allow for a substantive pathway to be created whereby teachers and students can connect across difference. In settings where there is a mismatch between the race of the teacher and the race of a majority of students, the frustration is compounded with what the new teacher believes to be the struggles in dealing with students and families, and so on, without having a vehicle to work through their beliefs and ideas, and the new teacher is driven further away from the profession. Considering the presentation of racial identity in the next chapter, white racial identity in particular is important, not just for the semantic moves to be understood, but also for the way in which the move of naïveté has long-term implications for students' opportunities based on the race of the teachers and the way in which students will be socialized by teachers.

Teacher education programs have a moral and ethical responsibility, if not to the pre-service teachers, then to the future students of these teacher candidates. The greater the turnover in a district, the less stable the teaching force, and the less students benefit from teachers who have developed their craft over multiple years. Additionally, when students are taught by those who have unexamined, naïve, and dysconscious racial identities and reasons for being teachers, there is likely to be an absence of culturally relevant pedagogy (Ladson-Billings, 1994).

Urban districts in the United States, which are nearly all re-segregated, have large student populations, recruit and hire many teachers, and have poor retention of new teachers, all of which results in maintaining a cycle of dysfunctional educational opportunities for students. Teacher education programs have the opportunity to break this cycle and to contribute to potentially greater teacher retention, and a more racially informed teaching force. Pre-service teacher preparation would benefit from a greater and sustained focus on examining the rationales of their pre-service candidates and helping the candidates to see the lack of substance contained within their rationales, and how such naïve rationales further situate pre-service teachers within color-blind frameworks. If teacher education programs sought to ensure that teacher candidates entered the profession with fully developed rationales for being teachers, armed not with a set of methods but rather a set of conceptual understandings of learning and a mechanism to help them engage both the desired conceptual understandings and the actual students in front of them, we might see the retention cycle of teachers change. A change in retention ultimately benefits students who are already subjected to the multitude of educational debts endemic to segregated public education. Further, and more importantly, teachers who have connected and full understandings of their rationales in place, the ones who have moved out from behind the shadow of color-blind orientations, are likely to engage in a culturally relevant praxis that recognizes the nature of systematic oppression in place for many K–12 students of color.

Chapter 6
White Racial Identity

In this chapter, I begin by presenting what I believe to be a set of three amalgamated assertions relative to White Racial Identity. I look at (1) participants' conceptualization of diversity as race, (2) how participants' white identity is linked to "racial others" rather than self, and then follow with (3) the incoherence of and/or under-developed nature of narrative relative to white racial identity. I present an analytical critique of Helms's White Racial Identity development model, proposing an alternate model of white racial identity.

Amalgamated Findings about White Racial Identity

Diversity as Race

An important element in beginning to understand white racial identity is understanding how people conceptualize race. In the case of this study, eight participants positioned "diversity" to serve as a coded synonym for race. Participants revealed most often that they understood diversity as race and consequently race as diversity, when asked to speak about the hometown in which they grew up. When we talked about each participant's hometown after the initial interview, I was curious to see in the second interview if the participants believed their hometown was diverse. In asking the question, I hoped to learn more about their hometowns and to understand how the students conceptualized diversity before asking any questions that specifically looked at race. I had not conceptualized asking the question of hometown diversity believing that participants would speak solely about race; understanding that diversity could be framed in a variety of ways and hold multiple meanings, I had expected answers from participants to touch on a variety of concepts to describe the diversity or lack thereof in each community. The first question of the second interview was, "Is your hometown diverse?" Without any additional prompting, most participants discussed diversity solely in terms of race and revealed an aspect of their socialized identity and orientation to the concept of diversity.

Pat, Angela, Bob, and Brian gave rather short answers directly stating their understanding of diversity. Pat responded, "Uhh, not really, the majority is probably white." Similarly, Angela responded, "No!" and when asked why not, Angela responded, "It is all white people." Bob asserted, "It's mostly Caucasian. I remember there were only three or four African Americans and maybe one Hispanic." Regarding his schooling experience, Bob said, "Uhh, yeah, actually for the most part [inaudible] when I got to high school it showed we had a substantial minority population." The quick responses of these participants established firmly that they conceptualized diversity along lines of race, and they succinctly linked the idea of diversity squarely to race in their responses.

Other participants, like Cathy, gave more extended responses when asked if their community was diverse. Cathy said,

> Uhmm, where I am from no. Where I am from it's very uhh, it's a lot of white kids and you don't get much, probably when I graduated ten-twelve African American students and then like a few Asians and that's about it, and there is not much diversity but in the city there is a lot more diversity.

In her response Cathy showed two important understandings relative to race; first, when thinking about diversity, Cathy saw diversity as an issue of race as exhibited in her statement that her town was "a lot of white kids." Second, what Cathy did not say is telling; in finishing the sentence, Cathy said, "You don't get much." While she did not fill in the blank, I would argue that she would have uttered "diversity" as her next word, particularly since she stopped herself from finishing, and then quickly said that she graduated with only ten-twelve African American students. If her claim was that there was not much diversity because it was white, providing information about the African American population appears to serve as an illustrative counterbalance to highlight that, in fact, the town was primarily white and, consequently, not diverse. Cathy also revealed that there was a geographic connection to race in that if one wants to find more diversity, one ought to go to "the city" as "there is a lot more diversity" in "the city." As previously seen in other respondents' answers, the link between geography and race is a common characterization.

Todd gave an entire racial profile of his county in order to explain his belief that where he grew up was in fact diverse. Todd asserted,

> Uhm, the county as a whole, I mean it's pretty diverse, we have like specific areas like Rampant and Fall Hills that are predominately African American and so is Highhack, and then where I live is mostly white like, and Mounthill is predominately Hispanic, so basically a good way to put it is through the parades we have. In Mounthill there is always Puerto Rican

Day Parade, in Fall Hills they have the Haitian Day Parade and in Bubbling Brook [where Todd lives] there is a St. Patty's Day Parade.

Todd clearly linked diversity to race and Todd was even able to provide a narrative tour of his county in order to clearly explain his point.

Barbara also provided a rather lengthy extended narrative to fully explain her position about the diversity of her community. Barbara stated,

> Shorefield, not so much, all white (lowers voice), and we had that urban-suburban program and they kept to themselves and we didn't know how to communicate with them so we couldn't really relate to each other and South Carolina I would say was a 50/50 split and then Mississippi I wanna say it was like 60/40 as white the minority but I noticed that everyone down South there wasn't very much cliques and that interests me.

Having lived in multiple communities, Barbara gave the racial breakdown of each in order to explain how she saw them as diverse. Like Todd and Cathy, Barbara also did some reduction of race to geography, presenting the urban-suburban program as some sort of Martian invasion and being unable to communicate with the students in the program. Having lived in Lilac a great deal of my life and having taught in Lilac, I know firsthand that the so-called urban-suburban program of which Cathy spoke really was a one-way street and only children from the city are sent to what is perceived to be superior suburban schools. There is no reciprocity to send children from elite suburbs to the urban schools, and the program has traditionally been predominately minority based. So when Barbara referenced the urban-suburban program, and considering the rest of her discussion, urban/suburban also became a proxy for race.

Interestingly, Barbara also exhibited some of the racial bonding language presented earlier in a different form; here she used it to highlight distinctions between "them," the racial minorities attending her school as a part of the urban-suburban program, and "we," the white students from her town. Barbara's distinctions are analytically interesting to me as I argue that it shows a sort of "white only" space stereotypically associated with Jim Crow-era segregation, and the we/them language supports a segregated distinction that appears to be relevant to thinking about the types of opportunities a future teacher sees as appropriate for white and minority students.

Part of Sierra's narrative response to this question presented earlier relative to white racial bonding bears repeating here, with additional information with which Sierra continued; it is not only illustrative of her conceptualization of diversity as race, but it also illustrates the larger narrative and societal construction that pathologizes race and was very much a part of Sierra's narrative. Sierra suggested,

> Not entirely, it is becoming more diverse, uhmm, there are two maximum-security prisons, and, you know, how prison populations are mostly Black.

So people move up to be closer to the families that are in prison so there
are lots of Black people but not a lot of Hispanics of Asian, just a small
Asian population in Sayville, but mostly Black and white. My high school
I think throughout my entire high school career there was a total of like
twenty-thirty Black kids is a lot out of fifteen hundred students and it
might be accurate or a little high, there was one Black kid in my French
class and a girl in my English and Chorus.

Like the others, Sierra's response limited the discussion of diversity to race and
codified her understanding of race as the direct link to diversity, or the direct
link to race as her understanding of diversity. Sierra also extrapolated more than
just a presentation of race in her response, as she revealed her belief and socialization about the lot in life of Black folks as primarily populating prisons and
having many Black people move closer to their prison-population family members. I believe that Sierra's narrative is not an isolated belief but rather part of a
larger community narrative. To try and understand Sierra's statement I investi-
gated the prison in her hometown. According to a *New York Times* article (1991)
regarding the state where Sierra lives, the prison population is nearly 80% African American or Latino despite the fact that in the state's total population less
than 25% are from the African American and Latino groups; this staggering
statistic helps to situate how Sierra arrived at her misinformed conclusions about
her community makeup as diverse mostly because of the prison. The Supermax
facility Sierra described was in fact cited by a federal judge in 1991 because
African American and Latino inmates were regularly "discriminated against in
discipline, job assignments and housing," according to a *New York Times* article
(1991). Minority inmates were able to prove they were disproportionately punished with longer and more severe sentences for in-prison violations, all of
which became part of the inmates' behavior record used to determine eligibility
for parole. Sierra did not go beyond "appearance" to reach her conclusion; in
fact, there are a number of social factors in place that speak to the complexity of
what Sierra articulated on the surface. That Black inmates are essentially perse-
cuted at this prison, having their stay extended beyond initial sentences, only
serves to reinforce Sierra's concept of diversity as race.

Steven appeared as the discrepant case among participants in terms of his
conceptualization of diversity. While he explained diversity as relative to race,
his confusing narrative did open up the realm of diversity beyond just race.
When asked if his town was diverse, Steven said,

Yes, very. Many different cultures and opportunities for many different
cultures and mainly because Lillywhite [the Ivy League school in his
hometown] is so popular and Ivyville has a lot of protests and stuff for
hippie stuff like a lot of nature stuff, Ivyville is gorgeous, if you're not into
that stuff but it's cool 'cause it's lots, different people and stuff for everyone. Our neighbors are from Honduras, I mean Puerto Rican Honduras,
and they are college professors and they are really down to earth.

In his narrative, Steven shifted to a discussion of his "Puerto Rican Honduras" neighbors and race became present in his conceptualization, but his understanding was clearly confused and confusing. However, perhaps given his way of illustrating diversity, the shift to the discussion of his neighbors did not seem to make a lot of sense. Also, in an attempt to talk about the community, Steven shifted topics from the "many different cultures" to the "opportunities," to the "hippie stuff," to the landscape and environment, and then back to "different people;" he often inserted undefined "stuff" into his response, thus confusing the ability one might have to follow his logic and description of how he viewed his home city as diverse.

White Identity and Its Link to "Others"

For many of the participants, questions asking about their whiteness produced responses that illustrated their understanding of their whiteness by discussing racial others, their whiteness, or really even themselves. For seven participants, discussing experiences of their own whiteness produced narratives that focused on others. Barbara talked about learning she was white by going to a so-called Black mall, and stated,

> One time when we were in Mississippi and we were kind of interviewing schools so we visited all the schools and one school the girls said there was one mall, the Bomba, and don't go there it's bad and we were like, why is it bad? and we went and it turned out we were the only white people in the mall and we didn't care because we're not like that, but the problem was all the Blacks looked at us and eyed us down and looked at us like, why are you here, and I was like, wow.

In her narrative, not only did Barbara link white identity back to others, but she essentially did not engage the question; she ignored really discussing herself and focused instead, in an implied manner, on how the "Blacks" created a racist situation by that fact that they "looked at" and "eyed" down Barbara and her mother. Also consistent with her narrative of expansive goodness and non-judgmental behavior, Barbara inserted that "we didn't care because we're not like that." For one to believe Barbara one would have to suspend in the mind's eye that this is the story she used as an illustrative example of knowing her whiteness. That this is the story she tells leaves open the strong possibility that "it"—race—did in fact matter.

When asked if she had experiences where she really knew she was white, Angela said, "When I went to a city school for the first time I was like, WOW! I am the white girl, like when I went for my placement last year and I was the minority and that's really different." It took what appeared to be Angela's first experience as the racial minority to understand that she was white. Angela did not consider other experiences that taught her that she was white. Angela spoke somewhat to the invisible nature of whiteness as being something that is not recognized as present without the counter-example to awaken the invisible part of white identity and make it known.

Unlike Angela, Steven essentially did not answer the question. When asked, "Can you think of an experience where you knew you were white?" Steven used the question as an opportunity to discuss and state his beliefs and positions about people of color.

> Uhmm, yeah, definitely. I started off knowing that the Black kids were nice, one was my age and one my sister's age, but then you got to high school and kids that got kicked out of school and I didn't. I had a different viewpoint of what the kids are 'cause they just don't care about anything.

In his narrative, Steven began with a strong "Uhmm, yeah, definitively," indicating that perhaps he had a particular, specific, or memorable experience. As his narrative continued, it became clear that he was neither going to answer the question nor do the work of understanding his own white racial identity. Instead of answering the question or exploring himself, Steven laid out an indictment of Black kids, insinuating that in his youth he "started off knowing that Black kids were nice," but then learned they were not because they "got kicked out of school" and "they just don't care about anything." His response and lack of willingness to engage self highlights the pervasive way in which White Racial Identity can both go unexplored and be actively avoided by white people simply through deflecting any conversation about self as white to racial "others" who can bear the brunt of the responsibility.

For Bob, Brian, and Todd, sports and teams with racial minorities were the experiences where they really knew they were white. Brian's narrative, presented earlier to show the conflict between Brian's claim to be open and non-judgmental despite his judgments, essentially claimed that he understood himself to be white by seeing "inner-city" kids (a proxy for not white) with pants worn low and "shorts that are too long" who "interacted" differently from him and his other white teammates. In a similar type of narrative Bob, said,

> I guess more so in basketball when I got towards seventh and eighth grade my school always played inner-city schools and they were allll Black and I started realizing not so much that you know I was just a different skin color and that but I started to notice they had a little more slaaaaang talk and they always definitely jumped higher than I could and they were fast you know and we always got our butts kicked by them and I guess sports is really just the place where I realized I am a white boy – I can't jump and I can't run.

Todd had a slightly different, albeit ultimately similar, narrative about sports that Brian and Bob had. Todd gave the following extended response:

> In eighth grade, when I started playing for St. George's, which was my school but my eighth grade school didn't have a team so I played for St. Paul's which is down in Highhack about five minutes away but it's like in the ghetto, and I was one of three white kids on the team and I hung with them and they were cool with me but then I started being friends with those kids and we would play basketball not for the team but at the rec center and at the center I had never been there but they lived in the neighborhood and I lived like five minutes away and one day I had my mom drop me off and none of my buddies were there, and there must have been sixty or seventy kids older and younger running around and I was the only white person and I was kind of just looking around and it wasn't until one of my buddies came that I got on a team cause no one wanted to pick a white kid, and I was pretty good and everyone stated calling me "white boy" and one kid was like, "Yo, white boy, I don't mean to call you white boy but I don't know your name," and it was like all the time from eighth grade until twelfth grade that was common for me when I played basketball I was one of the few white kids there and all the time you know you are white and then, like, I played in a couple of summer leagues and they have street announcers that would comment and I always got references to white guys and famous white guys or something.

Todd's narrative presented less judgmental language of the references by which he understood his whiteness, but, like the other narratives, the concept of his whiteness was predicated on racial others who served as the socializing orientation to understanding his whiteness. In this sense, it is racial minorities who not only suffer from the effects of white racism and white supremacy but who also bear the brunt of teaching white people that they are white. In a sense, the idea of learning that one is white via racial others is exploitative and demonstrates that white racial identity can be misunderstood by white people while simultaneously being completely ignored, without minority group interaction.

Sierra presented a similar response to Angela's earlier narrative, when asked if she ever had an experience where she knew she was white; she described an experience where she was one of few white people:

> I think like when I had an apartment on East Main Street and I was one of five white people in my building and I was uneasy because I had never really been around Black people before but they were the best neighbors I ever had and it was a great sense of community and everyone looked out for everyone and it changed my perspective.

Sierra also demonstrated the idea that white racial identity is predicated on racial others when asked if her whiteness shaped the way she teaches. After a twelve second pause, her response was,

> If I were to teaching in a suburban school it would be fine, but in the city
> they will be like, "White teacher, what do you know about us?" I had a
> friend who had an observation at a city elementary school and they were
> like, "Go back to the suburbs you don't know anything about us," and I
> don't want them to look at me like that and that's how they are going to
> look at me at first being a white teacher and wanting to teach in that envi-
> ronment makes me very aware of my whiteness and my perceptions of
> other races because I do not want, I don't want to convey negative percep-
> tions that will push them away from me and there are certain things about
> my upbringing and things that come from that and I need to think about
> how they play out in my interactions with people.

Clearly in this very lengthy narrative, Sierra transferred much of the onus for her
"whiteness" and its potential effects onto hypothetical racial others. Sierra
demonstrated that she had come to certain conclusions about what students from
other racial groups would do and saw racial identity as something only significant in a setting where her race differed from that of her students. Sierra's WRI
may be more developed than that of her peers in this study as suggested in
Helms's model (1984, 1990, 2003) because she acknowledged some ownership
in her experiences. In her housing situation, she highlighted that while the experience of being few among many shaped her understanding of her whiteness, she
also acknowledged that she went into the situation with judgments, and the experience helped to challenge some of the beliefs she had prior to the living situation. That she was able to see the experience as even slightly transformative is
potentially promising; in terms of the scope of this study, she is by far the discrepant case with regard to having the experience of being the only white, and it
served as a transformative "intervention" of sorts between her belief system and
the reality that the belief system ignores. Sierra was also cognizant that being a
youth with a parent whom she described as being like Archie Bunker had great
impact on her WRI development. While Sierra was misguided in many aspects
of her narrative and had generalized what potential responses could be from
purely hypothetical urban students, she did recognize that her "upbringing"
would impact the way she interacts with students of different races. While Sierra
did not recognize that those same socialized beliefs play out in settings with
other white students, she was the only participant able to problematize her white
supremacist racist upbringing, and bring to bear her experience on what might
be her White Racial Identity.

Incoherent and Under-Developed WRI Narratives

The last assertion that forms part of this amalgamated finding is that in participant narratives relative to white racial identity, white participant narratives appear to be incoherent and/or under-developed when addressing white racial iden-

tity. In part, these incoherent and under-developed narratives seem to indicate a certain level of uneasiness with the concept of participant whiteness and the implications of one's whiteness.

Angela's narrative presented a classic example of incoherent narrative as discussed by Bonilla-Silva (2006). Angela talked about not having a teacher from a different race until she reached college; she had one African American professor in her three and a half years at Righteous College, and when she was asked if that experience was in any way memorable, Angela said, "Yeah. Not really. No! I don't know? I don't think so?" In a sense one could look at the question and response and assert that the response is not a direct reflection of her white racial identity. I argue, however, that Angela's inability to reflect on the experience of having an African American professor, her first teacher of color in twenty years, and her inability to express what the experience meant to her as a white person, reveal that Angela is probably not in the habit of thinking about her whiteness or how her experiences are shaped by her own whiteness. If Angela is unable to think about her whiteness relative to the context of others, a typical manner in which participants attempt to make sense of whiteness, it is likely she is unable to think about her whiteness independent of such experiences. Relative to this smaller assertion of racial confusion, Angela took nearly every position one could take in answering the question, without ever definitively addressing the substance of the question.

Barbara seemed both amused and confused when asked if she identified as white, and her response engaged in the multiple-answer approach like Angela's, saying, "I guess. Yeah. I don't know. What else would I be (laughing)?" Also, when asked to talk about how her whiteness could impact her teaching, looking very confused and puzzled by the question, Barbara said, "That is a good question. I have never thought about it." Like many of the participants, Barbara had not openly thought about her own whiteness and the impact of said whiteness on the act of teaching or in terms of the very routine and mundane ways in which she lives her life, despite the dysconscious presence of her race.

Steven gave a confusing answer about his whiteness that avoided directly addressing the question and consequently directly addressing any aspect of his whiteness. When asked if whiteness shaped the way he taught, Steven said, "No, I have good morals and values and I want to be there for my kids and I don't care if they are Black, white, or whatever." In this response, Steven implicitly acknowledged a belief that if he were to engage his whiteness as significant, he would consequently present himself as a racist without "good morals and values." Steven also shifted the question back to students' race, thus avoiding the opportunity to think about the role his own whiteness plays in his socialization and experiences as a white in society that has been premised on white supremacy and racism.

Like Steven's, Brian's unexamined and confused narrative also ignored an engagement with discussing his own whiteness and speculating about hypothetical students. When asked if his whiteness shaped the way he taught, Brian stated,

> I would say just not being as, I don't know how to say it, as diverse growing up knowing one thing and someone else grows up knowing a completely different thing and there is a gap and how you fill the gap is kind of like your push to diversity, and I just, I don't know. The things that relate to the adolescents themselves on the individual level and talk about a TV show that would bridge the gap instead of saying you're African American so let's talk about Africa today and that would be completely obvious treating them like, yeah you're Black. But, it doesn't matter.

Brian's narrative was confusing as he jumped from topic to topic, with no topic directly addressing the question asked. In one sense, he claimed that his whiteness was akin to not being diverse when he said that he "would say just not being as . . . as diverse," and he struggled to conceptualize this as he was unsure of "how to say it." We have seen previously this idea of diversity as race and white people apparently being diversity neutral and other races being diversity engaged.

Brian went on to suggest that part of the task is to minimize the importance of race and that African American students would be engaged more by talking about a television show than talking about Africa and that the only reason a hypothetical teacher would even engage in a discussion of Africa would to placate African American students. One might assume that Brian, as a future social studies teachers, would want all his students from any racial group to know a lot about Africa. Knowledge of Africa seems extremely important for all students given what we know about human development and how much of our human existence is believed to be traced back to Africa. It is understood that the most racial diversity in the world exists in sub-Saharan Africa, for example, and many of the origins of all racial groups can be traced back genetically to the African context. Brian implied that he would not want to teach "Africa" to avoid appearing that he is teaching only to or for African American students, yet this position, which appears to be to protect his vision of self as expansive, missed the larger teaching opportunity and, in any case, was completely devoid of a discussion of his very own whiteness and its implications.

Pat deflected from whiteness and toward the idea that she is a presenter of material and curriculum and, as such, has to ensure that her whiteness is not a part of her teaching. When asked about the role of her whiteness and her teaching, Pat stated,

> I don't think. I'm just. I don't know how to say this. I want it to be about teaching and that kind of thing and there is no way to be objective when you are teaching, it's just impossible so I think things are gonna come out, but if you are like students are like white, it's just. I'm just gonna try not to tell that, come out, it shouldn't matter. I have this material I need to

teach you and sorry if you don't like it, this is how I grew up and so don't judge me because I'm white just like I won't judge you no matter where you are from.

Pat's narrative was extremely confusing, and like other participants, Pat was not able to really present a coherent or developed sense of her white identity; the confusion indicated a disconnect between what participants wanted to hold as dysconscious and questions that were asking them to directly and consciously address race. In her narrative, however, Pat did reveal a number of interesting concepts. First, she argued that teaching should be about material and consequently implied that her race should not be a part of that discussion. Pat also jumped again to hypothetical students, whom she already perceived as judging her. In her hypothetical defense of self, she also revealed that her whiteness "is what it is," a neutral concept, and that she just grew up that way, but she also made an interesting claim when she argued, "I won't judge you no matter where you are from." In that statement, Pat revealed her understanding that one's race is synonymous with one's geographic location, an interesting argument about racialized spaces and ultimately who belongs where.

On the more "unexamined perspective" end of this finding, Bob was asked to what extent his whiteness might shape his teaching. After a five-second pause, he said,

Uhhmm, I don't really know. I don't really, to be honest. I don't really know because I never really thought when I was a teacher I don't think Black, white, whatever, I just see them as a teacher and you are the leader of the group and you are what they need to respect and listen to and trust and just because I'm white I wouldn't change anything. I'm there to make sure these kids get the proper education.

Bob appeared not to have really thought much about his white racial identity and communicated that clearly in the front end of his response. Bob saw himself as "the leader of the group" and wanted students to not only "respect and listen to" but also to "trust" him. Bob was interested in teaching in an urban environment, and given the segregated landscape of the United States' urban schools, this means that Bob would likely be working with students who do not share his race. It is analytically ironic then that Bob saw his whiteness as a "just" case, as though it was a neutral element of his identity that he just happened to have and that his whiteness did not or would not affect anything in his teaching. Given the history of public schooling and the educational debt attached by white people to children of color, what reason would the students have to trust Bob? Bob had not done the self-interrogatory work of understanding not only the complexity of his whiteness but also the social history of his whiteness. From a culturally relevant standpoint (Dixson, 2005; Dixson and Fasching-Varner, 2008; Fasching-Varner & Dodo Seriki, 2012; Ladson-Billings, 1994), it is unlikely that without opening his own experience up to interrogation, Bob is unlikely to be able to engage students in a culturally relevant manner that would create a situation where students would want to respect him.

In an extended response to the question of how whiteness might affect or shape his teaching, Todd attempted to work through his understanding of whiteness. After a ten second pause, Todd said,

> That's a good question. Is my whiteness gonna shape the way I teach? I guess it won't affect it; if I am in a predominately white suburban school it will just be another day around white kids, but if I'm in an urban school that is probably the first thing they will see and I will have to prepare myself to defend against adversity because I'm white and if I'm in an urban or higher-needs school students won't like me because I'm white and how I deal with that I haven't thought about it and how well do you prepare for that. I honestly don't know and it's good to think about. Don't get me wrong but I'd rather not talk about my race because it is irrelevant to me teaching them, I think?

Todd's response showed that, overall, he had a fairly under-developed and confused sense of his white identity, as evidenced that he saw his whiteness only at the level of phenotype in his assertion that for students of color it "is probably the first thing they will see." Furthermore, Todd viewed whiteness as a "default" and as only relevant when dealing with kids who are not white, that is, in a "white suburban school it will just be another day around white kids." Like several participants, Todd linked race to geography, as the example of suburban to white and urban to high needs as signified codes (Hall, 1997) to represent children of color. Because Todd did not delve deeper than phenotype, he was unable to look at a systemic analysis of how whiteness was privileged in his own experiences growing up or how whiteness receives privilege in general, or to examine the systematic nature of white hegemony that has dominated the United States social landscape. Not only had Todd not actively thought about his whiteness, he also indicated that he had no desire to think about his whiteness and in a sense admonished me in telling me that he did not want me to get him wrong, but according to him, "I'd rather not talk about my race because it is irrelevant to me teaching them, I think?" The "I think" was a leveraged form of discourse that Todd used in an attempt to find out from me if what he was saying was the right answer; what is interesting is that like Bob, Todd's active refusal to think about, let alone problematize his whiteness, in all likelihood will block him from real engagement with students, particularly those students who do not share Todd's white privilege.

Cathy's exchange relative to her whiteness was perhaps the most unique and most illustrative for me of the concept of having an under-developed and critically confusing narrative about one's whiteness. Below is the exchange between Cathy and me.

Kenny: Can you think of an experience growing up where you knew you were white?

Cathy: (eight second pause) I don't think so. I grew up in a white area and so . . .

Kenny: . . . Any experience that showed you that you are white?

Cathy: If I did, I don't know about it, my parents might but, but I never thought anything of it. When we grew up there was nothing wrong with it, so.

Cathy's response missed the boat completely. To suggest that I would have to speak to her parents to know if she had an experience where she realized that she was white seemed to me, at least, to indicate that Cathy had not reflected or thought much about her own identity as a white person. Earlier we saw that when Cathy grew up, she had the experience with the "chocolate man" and her grandmother; Cathy clearly was able to talk about race to some degree throughout her interviews. What Cathy ended up articulating was a belief that the question implied "badness" as an attached value to whiteness, and that she felt okay with her whiteness growing up and consequently, to think about it now could disrupt that very narrative of goodness on to which Cathy held. Consequently, Cathy was unable to share any information that really or directly addressed the nature of the question. To that extent, Cathy's understanding of her own whiteness appeared, at least, to be under-developed, and the narrative was rather confusing to understand.

The importance of understanding the nature of unexamined whiteness, presented in confused narratives, is that such narratives appear to be an indicator that issues of one's white privilege, the history of whiteness, white supremacy, and white racism have also gone without consideration, and a conflict exists between what would be presently conscious and what is presently dysconscious. Any future educator who grew up in the post-Brown and post-civil rights era most likely was not socialized to the outwardly racist manners of times past, and consequently whiteness as a construct may have appeared to be outside of her or his view, but not in an unconscious way. Of the nine participants, only Sierra articulated that she was raised around notions of white supremacy. None of the participants went to public spaces with white- and Black-only bathrooms or water fountains as the nature of racism shifted from a violent, outward gesture of hate to a more silent yet equally violent, introverted racism that ultimately shares similar end goals albeit in a different outward manner. That participants were not socialized in an era of open ideological hate does not mean that, as white people, they have been free from the racist underpinnings that created Jim Crow segregation; their responses in the previous two chapters and those of this chapter show this to be true. In fact, an ideology of white supremacy is still socialized and taught; the workings of such an ideological system, however, appear in less visible, tangible, and open ways. Given that the ideology and structural systemic advantage of white people is still present and thus socialized, coupled with unexamined white identity, leads me to see a powder keg of dysconscious racial naïveté, volatile and virulent in nature, but now under a thinly veiled surface of invisibility, and still taught and socialized to future generations. Without intervention in this process, particularly with educators whose work is understood to be that of agents of socialization, each subsequent generation of white people is likely to develop deeper levels of unexamined white identity and deepened socialized racism that will be further coded, less visible, and more deeply couched in expansive language of inclusion.

Kenny and White Racial Identity

As a precursor to locating the participants in this study within the Helms model, I present some data relative to my own white racial identity. I did not interview myself using the same protocol given to the pre-service teacher participants in this study. As I am no longer a pre-service teacher, many of the questions would not have been germane to the discussion of my own white racial identity, since I have taught and have had a longer opportunity to engage in the work. As such, there were areas of the findings where my auto-ethnographic data did not fit, since the frame of the questions was intended for participants earlier in their career. As discussed earlier, for research that examines race, and in particular for white researchers examining race, our own narratives must be present in the work so that our work is not an examination of others with ourselves as neutral researchers, not implicated in the white supremacist social project. I am a white male and benefit from my whiteness in profound and deep ways. As such, it is important to see how my own experiences are both situated with, and replicate, whiteness and white supremacy.

I have shared my own color-blind orientations, and I want to problematize how whiteness benefits white people, including me, to the exclusion and punishment of racial others. Specifically, the goal for teacher educators like me is to establish that even having had more time in the profession does not absolve us from the responsibility of our orientations and actions premised upon, and situated within, a white supremacist framework. In fact, I argue that the matter of time may necessitate a heightened sense of scrutiny.

While I have tucked into my outward narrative about my own teaching that I enjoyed my teaching settings and believed that all children can learn, I spent the first three to four months in my first job as a fourth-grade teacher in urban Lilac feeling very skeptical, and waiting for my socialized stereotypes about deficient and uncaring urban families to manifest themselves. During the interview process for that first job I recited very cliché conceptualizations similar to those of participants in this study, and talked about how I saw my role as helper, and how much I would love the opportunity to work in the city given that I grew up in Lilac and went to Lilac schools. I did go to Lilac schools, and did have very positive experiences with students and teachers of color, yet being socialized around racism also internalized racist orientations that placed people of color within deficiency lenses. At some root level, below the outward abstract liberal orientation I presented to those hiring me, I believed the master or stock narratives (Delgado, 1993) would have to be proven true. I began the year waiting, each and every day, and believing that this would be the day when the myths and stereotypes would be proven as truths. This orientation made sense after twenty years of socialization around racialized beliefs through which I had been trained to keep my real beliefs hidden and to only express niceties outwardly. What I found, however, became what really propelled the first shift in my white racial identity development away from what Helms (1992a) cites as reintegrationist beliefs, centered on negative stereotypes, to a real challenging of what were comfortable racist beliefs, typical of the pseudo-independence status of white racial identity.

The families of the children I taught were wonderful, the community support was robust, the parents cared about their children's future and looked to the school to live up to their purported role in educating children, and the students were kind, wonderful, smart, and present with a very high, nearly 99%, attendance rate. Most of the parents attended the first open house in October, a situation that subsequently I would not find to be true in my experience in my suburban teaching. Most of the parents who did not or could not attend made provisions to call or make alternative arrangements to gather the information that was presented at the open house.

The children responded well to instruction, and flourished when given culturally relevant leaning experiences. When kids in the school appeared to be "acting out" it was almost always connected to problematic teacher behaviors, particularly with teachers who bashed students and families in the teachers' lounge and never really seemed to be about the kids themselves, but rather what the predominately white teachers attached to the children and their families. Despite how my socialization taught me to wait and look for the worst, I had to conceptualize a different paradigm, and that meant in part challenging my own white racial identity.

What I was waiting for was based in part on a base belief that families of color in urban centers were pathological, uncaring, and not interested in educating their children. The interviews in this study are startling because in many ways what the participants shared formed the basis of my own belief system that first year. What I also began to realize was that my own fears of being judged adversely by students and families of color, and wanting them to like me (Lensmire, 2008), affected my ability to fully understand my whiteness as I deflected onto students and families of color the paranoia and burden of my white racial identity in general, and my white supremacist racist beliefs in particular. Students and families could have judged me, and probably should have as the beliefs I took to the table were problematic. What I found instead was that at the end of the day, the students and families never really did judge me, or if they did, I never knew. They wanted to engage with me, and sincerely wanted me to engage with them. What emerged then was an orientation where I thought I could somehow hide or run from my whiteness, including the societal benefits I received as a white person, my white supremacist orientations, and my responsibility for the perpetration of racism. I attempted this white supremacist feat by using my guilty conscience to project onto families my own racialized beliefs and orientations of their deficiency, and the myths and stereotypes which actually formed the base of my white racial identity, and to which I had been socialized to believe as true.

While teaching provided considerable experiences to develop and grow a more evolved white racial identity, I would have to argue that, while each and every day proved that my socialization was wrong with respect to my beliefs about groups of people, somewhere in the back of my mind I always waited for the other shoe to drop, clearly a limit of my development as a teacher whose supposed commitment was to equity and diversity. When I left the classroom to pursue my doctoral degree, I was ultimately quite uninformed about race and relied on past socialization while trying to believe, well, "we (white people) really don't mean what we say and we're not that bad after all."

While I did develop healthy relationships with students and families of color, perhaps more healthy than many of my colleagues did, I wonder to what extent the perceived healthy relationships were really the reification of a patronizing act targeted to the students and families of color with whom I worked. Whereas I recognized my colleagues' discourses about students as problematic, I steadfastly believed that since I did not share their particular manifestation of a narrative, I was absolved from any implications surrounding white supremacy or racism. That I felt I was better than my racism inherently limited the authenticity of my relationships with those students and families.

During early coursework and professional experiences as a graduate assistant at The Ohio State University, I was actually propelled back to earlier statuses of racial identity. For example, as a graduate assistant field placement supervisor, I spent my first year responding to the white racial dog and pony show that rewarded white graduate students for participating in reifying whiteness; the benefits I received I can only now understand as being a co-conspirator in white supremacy through the teacher education (Fasching-Varner, 2009). As a supervisor in a teacher preparation program at OSU, I specifically sold out to being praised by the program manager and faculty coordinator for overlooking what were clearly racist orientations that guided the supervision of pre-service teachers in the education program that punished Black graduate students who were supervising student teachers. I let the rewards of whiteness blind me to what was going on in a classical sense of interest convergence (Bell, 1995a). It took changing advisors, intensive coursework, and some powerful scholars to awaken me to limits of my whiteness and to my complacent and simultaneously complicit role as a racist within the fabric of the OSU program.

Part of the work of unexamined white identity is keeping the unexamined identity hidden; this is the act of making race dysconscious in fact. For white people like me, a number of strategies are deployed to protect ourselves from having to deal with our whiteness. A major protection strategy is denial, and what I would call a malignant denial. The denial is malignant to the extent that our sense of self-protection creates situations where white people will deny the most awful of our white supremacist hate crimes to save face in the larger set of discourses (Brown & Levinson, 1987). Often very malignant denial is associated with so-called irrational hate groups such as neo-Nazis, the Klu Klux Klan, and Arian Nation members; an oft-heard malignant denial comes from those who deny the existence of the Holocaust of World War II that targeted Jews, Blacks, homosexuals, Gypsies, the mentally retarded, and other minority groups. Such denial could be seen as grand malignant denial, like a stage-four cancer that has grown beyond control. White people who do not present such grand malignant denial label those folks who espouse such denial as "irrational" and "virulent" as a way of locating themselves within a rational framework by distancing those who are framed as irrational. It is the less grandiose forms of malignant denial, however, that perpetrate the daily workings of white people, and which serve to protect unexamined whiteness.

In the past few years I have been confronted with some situations that not only illuminated my own struggle with my white supremacy and racism and consequently my white racial identity, but also were incidents that I (sub)consciously denied to protect and preserve my self-image as a good, rational, nice person who is non-judgmental, and so on. I attended Breezy Middle School, an urban middle school, which had approximately two thousand students in the sixth, seventh, and eighth grades at the time. In the sixteen years since I graduated from middle school, my denial of issues with race and ethnicity have helped me to spend little time or attention on my experiences and to at least dysconsciously let go of much of that time period in my life.

One such instance happened several years ago when I taught a course required of all pre-service teachers at Righteous College called Diversity, Social Justice, and Education. The students were non-traditional as teacher candidates in that they already had a bachelor's degree in a non-educational related field and had decided to switch careers and become teachers. These teacher candidates were different from the more traditional undergraduate students who formed the participant sample in this study as they attended classes full-time for one year and received a master's degree in education; additionally, they were eligible for state teacher certification where Righteous College is located. I spent time preparing the syllabus, carefully choosing readings and organizing the course around the interrelated concepts of equity, understanding self as raced/classed/gendered/sexualized/abled, and interrogating dominant discourses; my orientation in preparing the course as such becomes ironic given the event which I recount.

On the first night the fifteen adult students came in and sat down. I gave my usual talks about the course requirements and policies. and did some introductory exercises, and shared my vision for the course. At the break students appeared overwhelmed by the approach and workload and I would say half left the room, likely to console each other and complain about what was being asked of them. A few stayed behind in the room, and one young woman said in disbelief, "You don't remember who I am, do you?" I apologized and said that I really did not know who she was, and asked her to share how we knew each other. In the moments that followed I had to take responsibility for the effects of my whiteness and how my whiteness and white identity privileged my experiences with negative consequences for those whom my whiteness and white supremacy targeted.

Ana asked me, "Did you go to Breezy?" I responded that I did and Ana proceeded to tell me,

> I really don't know how I can take this course with you, it's pretty messed up really that you of all people would be teaching a course in diversity; I was in your class and we both applied to go to Alternative High, both got interviewed, I got in and you didn't. You and the other two white boys that didn't get in tormented me for the rest of the school year. The last month of school was awful and you said that I only got in to Alternative High because I was Hispanic and that hardworking people like you get punished for being white, and if it was based on work quality and intelligence you should be going there and not me. I will never forget those words! The words you and those other boys used haunted me all four years at Alternative High—I always asked myself, why am I here, did I not deserve to be here? Now you are supposed to teach me about diversity and your whole talk about getting to know yourself—it all seems like crap, you don't even know who you are. How could you forget the way you treated me?

Alternative High was presented to the community as a school without limits and without walls. The borders and divisions typical of schools do not exist at AH. The school at the time had a student population of about one hundred fifty students; in Lilac the average population of the five city high schools was between fifteen hundred to two thousand five hundred students. AH was vastly different in this sense; at the time, students had freedom to come and go as they pleased, eat meals in classes, call teachers by first names, and create courses of study based on interest, and the school was exempt from state testing and did not use report cards with grades but rather narrative feedback. While AH has since changed, at the time it was "the school" families wanted their children to go to and there was a lengthy interview process that included interviewing teachers, and the students themselves, amongst a host of other criteria. The myth at the time that my parents had told me was that AH used racial and ethnicity quotas and that of the forty new freshman students only one or two would be white and male. What I know now was that the school took the students who, during the interview process and based on teacher recommendation and interviews, were best suited to the school. While I cried foul and used meritocracy, at the end of the day, Ana's acceptance to AH and my rejection from AH show that I, in fact, was not the deserving of the two students, and the merit I perceived was a coded way of projecting my whiteness without the responsibility or need to call it such.

In an instant my whole world changed. Ana was right; the dysconscious quickly moved to conscious. As I regained consciousness of the events and put the pieces together, I felt numb. I remember articulating all the ideas that Bonilla-Silva (2006) talks about as being color-blind and based in a false sense of merit. I was the child of an immigrant; my mother spoke English as a second language, I could have and should have been a different person, I had reasons to do and be different, but I ultimately did not and was not. In our house whiteness took precedence. My mother actively refused to teach me German, and I could be read for what I was—white—with all the privileges that are associated with whiteness. I had no basis to judge Ana or think that she was less deserving than I was to go to Alternative High. Clearly she more deserved to go there as she was chosen and I was not. The white supremacy, racism, and myths/stereotypes about minorities that I had been socialized to believe as true helped to create a situation where my whiteness was directly lodged as a weapon. It forced me to have to acknowledge that, at best, I could be an antiracist racist (Clark & O'Donnell, 1999) and, while my current narrative and theoretical understandings of race, diversity, and multiculturalism help me work with educators, I had not done the very basic work of understanding my own whiteness in a meaningful way. If I was to continue to see myself merely as an anti-racist I had to keep doing the work that Ana intuitively understood as hypocritical—telling teachers to do things I was not willing or able to do myself. In claiming the position as an anti-racist racist I could at least, for the first time, look systemically at my implicit and complicit roles in the white supremacist domination that has marked and continues to mark the landscape of the United States. While I may have been more informed academically, the concept of race is a lifelong struggle, and I understood that my status as a racist white could never, will never, and should never, disappear. To assume it would disappear or was no longer relevant, which is how I was living my life when I re-met Ana, would mean that in fact I was still perpetrating the very racist actions against which I attempt to teach teachers to fight—being racially dysconscious. In a profound and ironic twist Ana helped me to understand the shortcomings of the white racial identity model's linear progression; Ana was exploited by me, as my learning came at the social cost of her having to take a class in anti-oppressive education from one of the very people who oppressed her.

Ana and I discovered a number of anomalies in our experiences post-middle school that show the tangible effects of racism. I went on to become fluent in Ana's native language of Spanish as I had opportunities while in college to live in Spain and Chile, whereas Ana explained that she lost a lot of her Spanish as she was socialized to believe, by my white racism and that of others, that her Spanish was not a valued commodity, but rather a marker of difference used to judge her. Ana finished high school and went to college, always feeling that she had to prove herself to white people and that there was an under-current form of

narrative from someone—a Kenny, let's say—who was judging her and believing that she did not deserve to be there.

On the other hand, I flourished in college just by being white; "Kenny" learned quickly to manipulate his whiteness for its benefits, learning how to use office hours to ingratiate himself to professors, telling them how much he was learning and how great their classes were. I also was able to manipulate my working-class upbringing as a means of receiving sympathy from faculty while hiding behind the privilege and never really acknowledging it.

I went on to teach children and then to leave the classroom to educate future teachers on how to do "the work." I eventually focused on Critical Race Theory and multiculturalism to complement my literacy background, hoping to prepare teachers to better serve populations who have received the least from the education system. Ana, meanwhile, entered a career in social work and saw how children from her Latino community in Lilac and other groups of color were being mistreated by a white teaching force, and also by the narratives and actions of white people in the community bent on punishing children and families of color. Ana decided she needed to enter the system to help create a different set of narratives, to help protect students of color from people like me, the Kenny whose whiteness, along with that of other white people, helped to shape two trajectories in two lives that took twists and turns and ultimately brought each back to the other. In the weekend class, it was Ana who taught me, and ultimately the students benefited from an honest and open discussion of the experiences that Ana and I shared throughout the course, trying to understand the complex trajectories of our raced lives.

White Racial Identity within Helms's Model

In combination, the participants' color-blind approaches, white racial bonding, conceptualizations of race as diversity, deflection of whiteness to racial others, and white people's confusing and seemingly under-developed narratives give some insight into where the participants might appear to be in Helms's White Racial Identity model. I will ultimately argue that the model itself is an extremely limited analytic for understanding whiteness in a more systemic or global way, but I first must present where in Helms's model the participants and I are located to give shape to what will be my critique of the model's utility.

The Contact Status—I'm Innocent

Brian, Barbara, and Cathy are the three participants who appear to embody the most characteristics and qualities associated with the Contact Status. Much naïveté relative to race exists in the Contact Status, and "the person does not consciously think of herself/himself as White" even though she or he may acknowledge that phenotypically she or he is white (Helms, 1992a, p. 37). When asked directly if she identified as white, Barbara most exemplified this quality as demonstrated by her response, "I guess, yeah, I don't know what else I would be," and then she laughed out loud. The lightheartedness with which Barbara described her racialized identity was consistent with someone early in the Contact Status, where race has not been part of the person's active and conscious thoughts and potentially a great deal of work, such as denial, has been put in place to remain that way.

Brian and Cathy also struggled with self as raced, as is evidenced in Brian's reducing race to TV shows as his method to bridge the racial disconnect between himself and students. Cathy's confusion rested with whether she had ever had an experience where she knew she was white, and she suggested that her parents would be better suited to answer the question.

During the Contact Status one comes to know that racial groups exist, but color-blind discourse is used to "minimize differences in treatment due to race" (Helms, 1992a, p. 38). In explaining his understanding that television could be a better cultural connecter to students than race, Brian also asserted that with respect to one's race, "it doesn't matter," a very consistent attempt at providing minimalization of race. Barbara also emphasized the minimization of race in explaining that she "think[s] everybody is equal," and with her outright claims that she literally did not see race. Cathy, too, engaged in significant color-blind discourse, as presented earlier, and was quick to minimize race as exemplified in her belief that she taught the same way regardless of location, student type, or situation, believing that such an approach helped her to "show no bias."

The last quality associated with a white person in Contact is that she or he often has limited authentic positive experiences with people of color, at times using the person of color to teach the white person. Cathy was unable to distinguish between one's race, one's geographic location, and one's learning environment. Due to her limited experiences with people of color, and particularly her description of the small town as "a white area," I would argue that Cathy actually may have been in what I am conceptualize as "Pre-contact Status"; she was still attempting to learn the basic meanings and implications of race; for argumentation purposes I will say she was very early at the Contact Status with respect to the element.

Further evidence of Cathy's lack of experiences with people of color are found as she described only ever having a couple of minority students in her K–12 schooling experience; additionally, she made rather confused statements that she had lots of teachers from different races but then she described teachers' military service and high school performance as being indicative of having had teachers from a variety of races. Barbara's situation was different from Cathy's situation as she lived in ultra-elite suburban areas, considered self-contained in nature, and never had a teacher of color until college. In that one experience, she felt like she learned a lot about people of color and thought that the experience was "cool" because "you just don't see it," referring to Black teachers; her presentation of only her negative experiences with minority students from the urban-suburban program indicated limited positive experiences with people of color. Barbara's one positive experience became the vessel she used to carry information about the whole race. Brian shared that in his formative schooling experiences there were "maybe three Black (lowered voice) kids;" he had no teachers of color, and his desire to teach around a population similar to him, which he described as "the suburban system . . . would be the easiest transition for me," showed his limited experiences with people of color, and consistency with the contact status.

Disintegration Status—How Can I Be White?

Participants Angela and Pat most consistently appeared to fit within the Disintegration Status. Disintegration Status revolves around "guilt and confusion"; realizing that there are differences between white people and people of color, the person tries to balance relationships with both groups (Helms, 2003, p. 50). With respect to White Racial Identity, Angela exhibited qualities associated with the Disintegration Status as she realized differences between white people and people of color. Her experience of being in a school with a predominately minority student population helped her to understand that differences in the opportunities offered to students existed, but ultimately she dismissed the situation as being "just the way it is," claiming that she would love to have a different perspective but that she is "just white." In a disintegrationist way, Angela tried to balance relationships with both groups, yet had not developed significant or meaningful relationships with people of color. Although racially overwhelming, Angela's field placement was a positive experience and she learned that she would like to work in that environment as she saw positive opportunities for students of color. Angela felt comfortable in the setting despite her initial reaction of "WOW! I am white," when she first entered the school.

Pat also attempted balancing relationships between both her white group and groups of racial others. In part she saw her experience with an African American professor as positive, but thought that the experience was positive because, from her perspective, "he didn't put his cultural bias" in the course. In another instance Pat wanted to believe that in her schooling the "racial slate was clean," a belief that helped place focus on students of color having positive experiences in school with white teachers; Pat also recognized that her teachers must have had "some pre-conceived notions" of students of color that did come into play when "there was a conflict" between white teachers and students of color.

A second component of disintegration is that white people often turn to other white people to seek resolution on feelings about race, and they learn that "when interacting with people of color, if he or she wants to be accepted by other White people, then he or she . . . must violate . . . moral and ethical principles" (Helms, 1992a, p. 46). With respect to the first aspect, Angela appeared bothered that students of color at Righteous College gave her and other white people a "vibe" about the lack of commitment to diversity. However, when asked if she attended events or programs that promoted diversity and could exhibit to students of color that white students do in fact have a commitment to diversity, Angela stated that she would rather not, asserting that she only went "freshman year when we had to." Angela did not feel a compelling reason to attend such events unless forced, and would rather talk to other white people about the effects of this "vibe" than talk to students of color about her perceptions of what she thought was the "vibe," or attend events and participate in a meaningful way that would reduce any rationale for this perceived "vibe." On one hand she felt put off by her perception of this negative vibe, but she was also unwilling to personally do anything about it. Angela's disinterest in attending events showed a moral conflict as she placed the onus on students of color for something in which she was not willing to engage directly with them, and she held them accountable for a feeling that she believed they had created, but which she had created in her mind.

As demonstrated in her earlier narrative about her interest in an African American student, Pat showed a similar disintegrationist perspective. First Pat sought resolution about the raced situation from another white person, her mother, who helped socialize Pat about race. Thus the resolution Pat sought would be consistent with the belief system she had already been socialized to believe as true. Pat also broke all moral and ethical principles in accepting the racist position that she should not pursue a relationship or discovery with the African American student. The stock stories (Delgado, 1993) from which her mother drew in helping Pat seek resolution and the idea that Pat's male family members needed to protect her present questionable racial ethics. Pat's male family member would not need to protect her from a white peer, but when the love interest is African American then there is a need for protection, certainly a racist supposition. Instead of doing what she thought was right, Pat deferred to what was white. Acceptance from her family was more important than developing a meaningful relationship free of bias and judgment with the African American young man. In accepting her mother's resolution, Pat favored what she was taught about race despite how such beliefs violated human morality and the basic principles of the human experience.

Reintegration Status—We Have the Best 'Cause We're the Best

Participants Bob, Todd, and Steven best fit within what Helms describes as reintegration. The Reintegration Status encompasses both covert and overt racist beliefs, with "hostility and anger directed toward people of color" (Helms, 1992a, p. 53). For Bob, hostility and anger were exhibited in his description of

Black kids' slang and the students of color having a perceived athletic ability more developed than his. Further, Bob's hostility and anger directed toward people of color were exhibited in his belief that it is "horseshit," from his standpoint, how much Black students get away with by using "the race card," and his inability do the same.

Todd's hostility and anger toward people of color was palpable. For instance, Todd expressed his assumption that he had to defend his whiteness to students of color in a manner that indicated he was angry about this, although he was speaking of hypothetical students. His hostility and anger were also evident in his perception that students of color would not like him due to his race, and his expressed view that students of color were something you "deal with." Even more pointedly, for Steven, there was an underlying hostility in his idea that students of color should not even bother coming to school as there was no point since they did not want to learn anyhow.

Negative stereotypes and a total denial of racism also generally characterize reintegration (Helms, 1984, 1990, 2003). Bob, Todd, and Steven all denied racism and the need for a focus on race, while simultaneously holding negative stereotypes about race. While claiming to be non-racist and non-judgmental, Bob used his experience playing basketball with students of color to promote a set of stereotypes about Black slang talk and Black athletic superiority; he used his experience in urban classrooms to characterize Black students as late, not interested in learning, and in need of more patience than their white peers due to the stereotypical attributes Bob attached to students of color. Steven denied that racism affected his own life or the lives of others and believed that all children need exactly the same thing in their educational experience, yet he conceptualized students of color very judged and stereotyped ways, as coming from deficient families with parents that do not value education. Todd believed that race is unimportant as a consideration in education and denied racism for himself and his family, justifying that his family's association predominately with white people was "the farthest thing from racist." Yet in describing his purported belief, Todd characterized neighborhoods of children of color in stereotypical ways, at one point describing a neighborhood as "ghetto." His speculative argument that "African American and Latino can be just as smart as white kids" implied that intelligence is only conditional, and is at times linked to race, a stereotypical view of racial inferiority as biological.

Pseudo-Independence—Why Not Just Become More Like Us?

The first eight participants presented themselves with attributes of statuses most aligned within the first phase, the abandonment of racism. Sierra was a discrepant case with respect to her white racial identity within Helms's model and presented more within the Pseudo-Independence Status (PIS); this second phase of the identity development model leans toward the evolution of a non-racist identity. In PIS, a shift in belief occurs as one begins "to acknowledge the responsibility of White people for racism and how he or she wittingly and unwittingly perpetrates racism" (Helms, 1990, p. 61). Sierra demonstrated characteristics of pseudo-independence not exhibited by other participants, and was the only participant who openly acknowledged her socialized upbringing as racist; she was able to talk about catalyst experiences, such as living in a predominately Black community, and taking courses that examined the psychology of race and examined the effects of race on birthrates and infant mortality, and helped to challenge the racist orientations of her upbringing.

Helms (1992a) believes that when a white is in the pseudo-independence status, she or he begins "to acknowledge the responsibility for the whys of racism" (p. 61), and what had once been comfortable racist beliefs are no longer comfortable. Sierra struggled with the conflict between the beliefs to which she was socialized and a newly emerging set of beliefs that were informed via other paradigms and approaches. So while Sierra did not believe that the new information she had learned and her positive experiences had replaced her racist orientations, she thought that the beliefs were at least challenged and was not sure what do with them. Sierra was beginning to acknowledge the role of her racism and was worried about how her racism would be read by students, a sharp departure from other participants who were worried that students would judge them as racist, a conflict to their auto-beliefs of being good non-judgmental people. So while participants in this study may have felt apprehension about what students would believe, Sierra was able to understand that she was in fact racist and had been socialized to be racist; consequently, if someone did judge her as being a racist, there would be a foundation within her experience that substantiated the belief.

Immersion/Emersion Status—I'm White!

I locate myself within the Immersion/Emersion Status (IES). The IES is when the white person is searching "for [a] personally meaningful definition of Whiteness and re-education of other White people about race and racism" (Helms, 2003, p. 52). This work requires that the white "person replaces White and Black myths and stereotypes" and reflects on the meaning and history of both whiteness and Blackness in the context of the United States (Helms, 1990, p. 62). This status is thought to be difficult to engage with because it requires that the white person "assume personal responsibility for racism and to understand one's role in perpetuating it" (Helms, 1992, p.74).

In the last phase of my doctoral program, I had the opportunity to participate in an urban middle schools research project where I was able to see the effects of my white privilege to some degree; for example, I was able to walk into a school as a graduate student without question or verification of my identity while the principal investigator of the study, a Black woman with a PhD, was practically asked to give a blood sample each and time we entered the building. Situations like this have helped me to reflect on the history of whiteness and Blackness within the landscape of the United States, a landscape that promotes repeated negative treatment along what can be understood only as lines of race. In the United States, my whiteness is a sort of super pass, whereas the principal investigator's race raised flags and served in juxtaposition to my race, as she was required to produce identification each and every time we entered the building although I never was asked for identification. Clearly reflected in the experience is a systemically internalized belief situated within the stock story of "fear" and "distrust" of people of color.

My scholarly areas of inquiry, Critical Race Theory and Culturally Relevant Pedagogy, have also helped to provide a theoretical tool kit in the process of assuming both personal and systemic responsibility for how racism works to my advantage and simultaneously to racial others' disadvantage. I was also socialized to different orientations that did not inherently privilege the white experience, but rather showed what a fraud my whiteness really is. My case in point was learning from Ana what my racism actually looked like and felt like to the victims of my racism, even though I now recognize that for Ana to have to show me my racism in effect further exploits Ana as a victim of my racism.

I also want to be explicit that conducting this type of research or providing self-disclosure is neither newsworthy nor honorable; it is simply the right thing to do and in fact what should be seen as a very ordinary and mundane action that privileged people do in an attempt to address the very nature of our privilege. The shift into this status of Helms's WRI model has inherently shaped the way I approach my teacher education courses and helped me to self-identify within the construct of being an anti-racist racist (Clark & O'Donnell, 1999). Further, an immersed/emersed white identity helps me to continually challenge where my assumptions and beliefs come from, and how these beliefs serve to privilege certain traditions and orientations.

Critique of the WRI Model

The descriptions presented in the previous section were an attempt at locating the participants of this project within the Helms (1984, 1990, 1992a, 1992b, 2003) model of White Racial Identity. Helms believed that the model could be helpful to white people, and recognized that since white people have identity, a model of identity development could be helpful for white people to address "unresolved racial development issues" (Helms, 1990, p. 53). While Helms did in fact examine real empirical narratives in her formulation of what would be the statuses, and in the early nineteen eighties worked with pre-service teachers, the scholarship with respect to WRI has remained largely a theoretical construct as opposed to a site of empirical examination. In gathering the narratives of the pre-service teachers for this research project I had hoped to contribute a more empirically situated look at the White Racial Identity model presented by Helms. Perhaps even as far as the conceptualization and proposal of this project, I had hoped to be able to use and understand the WRI model as a means of better understanding pre-service teachers and contributing to the work that teacher educators do. In the next section, however, I present what I believe are critiques of the WRI model and why ultimately the model, as it is, provides limited utility for educators.

The Model Is Just a Point of Reference

At best, the model and locating white people within the structure of the model are simply a point of reference. The idea of the model is premised on the presence of characteristics or attributes of particular statuses; thus, attempting to locate participants within the model is taking what you have learned about a white person, as in this case from participant interviews, finding out what characteristics appear in the articulated responses of participants, and establishing a point of reference about how the participants exhibit qualities x, y, and/or z. As researchers we are making what we intend to be educated attempts at locating participants, but ultimately what we present about the participants, WRI is just a point of reference. In this research, this point of reference is also heavily influenced by the lens that I bring to the examination of the interview transcripts. For example, if I read through the same participants' transcripts when I first knew Ana seventeen years ago, I most likely would have seen vastly different points in the narratives and probably would not have associated WRI characteristics in the same way.

In chapter 3 I explained the rationale for approaching this work through the idea of testimonial interviews, asserting that the power of such a methodological approach is the recognition that through her or his lens, any reader of the testimonial data could read and view the information differently from me. In fact, any reader of this book will minimally bring to bear a unique identity with respect to the interaction of race, gender, age, socio-economic status, sexuality, religion, political orientation, and a host of other identity elements that necessitate distinct understandings of the data. The jurisprudence system in many nations recognizes that people bring to bear a trajectory of identity to the word (testimony) and thus create systems requiring unanimous decisions among, say, twelve people. Clearly our jury system has its own unique and historical problems, many of which center on race, but the idea iss similar in this work–to recognize that my way of seeing the data should be at least plausible even when the reader brings differences to bear on the words of participants. To that end I too must be open to alternate explanations when the rationale provided by a reader is plausible.

While it may be interesting to see how participant A exhibits a particular quality associated with the Contact Status, how does it really inform us relative not only to the participant but to the participant within the larger societal framework where whiteness and white supremacy live? The answer is that the model becomes a relegation of whiteness and white identity away from the larger conversations about race, merely a point of reference about individuals, and consequently maintaining the conversation at the individual level. My argument is not that having a point of reference is necessarily a bad thing, but rather that the point of reference has to progress beyond the individual to look at the individual's placement within the larger societal framework, and it must be more than just a point of reference before anything transformative can arise.

Linear or Circular?—It Still Lives outside of White People

In earlier forms, Helms' model was presented linearly (Helms, 1984), but in later iterations, Helms (1994, 2003, for example) stressed the importance of recognizing the model in less linear ways. I think a dichotomous argument relative to the model about the linearity, or lack thereof, is ultimately less important than understanding how the model is actually situated as being inherently outside of the person and certainly outside of white people as a group. Despite Helms' clarifications I believe that the model is still a fairly linear concept, and to evidence this I would argue that it has a starting point, contact status, and an ending point, autonomy, with clearly delineated points in between. Even if not intentional, the model creates an understanding that the goal is forward movement. Even Helms (1990) claims there is opportunity for participants to move through, between, and circularly through the statuses; the ultimate goal is toward autonomy and thus presents a linear direction from contact as a beginning toward autonomy as an end.

In either case I would argue that the model as it is presented has the ability to be a structure that lives outside of the person. Again, as a point of reference approach, the model becomes about particular attributes exhibited by particular individuals. Thus individuals in such a model can make claim that their whiteness is not who they are but at best represents a limited set of characteristics that are attached to what they say, in this case during their interviews. Further, the possession of any attributes or characteristics is independent of other white people and independent of the global structure of white supremacy in general; as a white person I might argue that my characteristics do not seem as problematic as someone else's characteristics and so we do not share whiteness, which is often viewed as a bad thing by white people attached to the so-called irrational Jim Crow–era racists. A limit of this approach is that even if a white person recognizes the need to engage in thought about her or his status relative to the model, the model is relatively stable and she or he passes through status to status with the fixed model and is able to move progressively from start to end, from racially problematic to racially evolved. As a stable entity then, the model lives both outside of the person and outside of the collective experience of whiteness. Whether denying one's WRI altogether, or attempting to understand the identity by working through a static model, white people see WRI as living outside of them; a theoretical construct that does not represent who they are but rather tries to give shape to characteristics and locate such characteristic within particular statuses. What the model does not recognize is that WRI is an already/always condition, not a sometimes/then/now state. What this means is that WRI is something that white people already and always possess individually and collectively; the model itself should be seen as fabric that weaves together the trajectories of white people as opposed to the sometimes/then approach of "sometimes I was in contact, then I x, y, and z, and now I moved on to disintegration" approach.

So What? Who Cares?

Another critique of the model may be less about the model and more about how the application of the model is used by researchers. The idea that the model as a research tool can help researchers understand people's identity is a problematic orientation. At times, I am guilty of having perpetuated this problematic orientation. Initially I had conceptualized my research around the utility the model might have in terms helping me to understand where participants were within the model. So what? Who cares? As a project, the work of participants' identification within a model is frankly uninformative and does not recognize key points. First and foremost, understanding WRI is completely useless unless the participants have the opportunity to examine their own narratives and to think about their position within the model and the implications of their WRI. Looking at others without looking at one's self serves to perpetuate the very racist foundations against which the model is working, as seen with my interaction with Ana. When the project is conceptualized as such, very little is learned. In the case of this research, the opportunity to engage the participants was in a sense lost. Not only were the participants near the end of their teacher education program, but they were also not my students, and the research did not involve helping them to understand the ways in which their narratives indicated aspects of their (un)examined dysconscious WRI, which could have helped shape their practice. Working with pre-service teachers around unexamined and dysconscious WRI may have been a more interesting project; that was not, however, the project that was undertaken. So, a major flaw of the model is that unless the white people either individually or collectively examine their identities, all we are left with is the model that serves as point of reference, unable to provide structure for white people to self-interrogate and work against the white supremacist and racist nature of our whiteness, and open to the questions, so what? Who cares?

WRI is Over-Dependent on Self-Revelation and Lacks Nuance

The model becomes about what participants tell either themselves or in this case, tell me, as the researcher. As we saw consistently with every participant in this study, including me, there are aspects of our WRI that are denied, buried, and otherwise unexamined. There are also elements of our lives which we may be unwilling to discuss even when we do remember them so we make them dysconsciouss; there are other aspects of our identity that lie so deep they cannot enter into the discussion because they are simply absent from our conscious thought processes. In understanding this aspect of the critique, my argument is that when focused at the individual level, an inevitable part of the WRI process, the model lacks proper nuance. To explicate how nuance could be added at least at the individual layer, I am drawn to a rather old theoretical construction about individual identity, represented as a schematic originally described by Luft and Ingham (1955) as Johari's Window.

In this model, the first, or open, window contains aspects of ourselves that we reveal to others consciously; the open window reveals portions of our identity known to us and to others equally. We are aware of what we are sharing with society and what others know about us. This is the level of revelation in which the participants in this study engaged and it is what informed the location of their WRI which draws primarily from this open window and relies on what is self-reported. The WRI location of each participant does not actively consider other windows; as it is, the model is not necessarily a framework that considers what is contained within the other windows.

The second, or hidden, window contains aspects of ourselves that we choose not to reveal to others and while they are known to us, we consciously or dysconsciously keep what is behind that window from others. In sharing the Ana story, I shared something that had been kept behind my hidden window until it was shared with the class and until I wrote it; I moved it toward the open window because I believed it was critically important in understanding my identity. For other study participants, however, there were aspects of their WRI that I would not be able to ascertain given the nature of the knowledge behind the hidden window. Because the hidden window is not revealed, it is also difficult to know how much information is kept behind that window, and what is the proportion of information behind the window compared to what was revealed through the open window.

The third, or the blind, window contains public aspects of ourselves that we do not control. These identifying characteristics are not in our conscious sense of who we are. Because others can perceive these characteristics, however, they can be made available to us. This portion of our identity is a potentially contentious aspect of our identity because others attach value to these characteristics and we have much less control over this aspect of ourselves. In a sense participants were very apt to use the blind window as a means of laying out their judgments of people of color I can judge you but I will never tell you how or why. Particularly when the model is used by researchers to describe other white people's location within the model, there is a great potential with respect to WRI identity for researchers to bring too much to bear by means of their own perceptions of participants when thinking about their location within the model; our own subjectivities and positionalities (Peshkin, 1988) effect how we see participants. Participants do not get to control how they are read, nor do they have the opportunity to control how they are read by others. I very specifically attempt to balance the potential negative effects of the hidden window in presenting significant amounts of actual participant speech so that what I understood about participants was informed, as much as possible, from their own words. Because this research is shared, as this book, the second it is shared with anyone besides me, it is no longer mine, and any reader is also likely to apply a blind window to her or his reading of the work, and neither the participants nor I can control that aspect of this work.

The fourth and final window, the unknown window, contains aspects of self-identity of which we are not conscious. Although this source clearly motivates some or many of our behaviors, it is not accessible to conscious thought or external perception. Thus the great mystery becomes what we do not know about one's WRI, which is as important as what we do know. The unknown window signifies that even with careful attention paid to participants' words, or even a white person self-describing her or his WRI, the unknown aspect of our identity could create a space for a white person to appear one way in the WRI model yet really be located in a very different space or place. In my presentation of a different way of conceptualizing WRI, I will focus on recognizing that these four windows force a more complex understanding of WRI that moves beyond simple statuses marked by the "open window" characteristics self-presented by participants.

Moving beyond the Critiques

Critique is easy; in lodging a critique one can pick apart a particular construct and present everything she or he perceives wrong with the idea. It is far more difficult to take the critique and do something constructive with it. From the outset I wish to explain that my critiques of Helms's model are in no way intended to lessen the work of Helms with respect to WRI. A well-respected academic, clearly Helms is the most influential scholar on WRI in both the twentieth and the twenty-first centuries. Respect is owed to Helms's scholarship, which is considered to be the first and clearly most well-developed model of white racial identity. Recently the Supreme Court of the United States turned to her expertise in white racial identity in formulating opinions.

My critiques are not intended to do away with the need for or idea of the WRI model and, in fact, like Helms, I believe that having a model is at least one way to begin the process of examining what often goes unsaid by white people about our own internalized racism and the effects of our white supremacy on other groups. The desire for having a WRI model rests with the hope that white people can explore "the production and reproduction of dominance, subordination, normativitiy, marginality, and privilege" (Frankenberg, 2005, pp. 236–237). My critiques and consequently the model I propose are intended to help the examination of WRI live to its best and fullest intention, that of understanding the nature of whiteness, white supremacy, and racism as the "product of local, regional, national, and global relations" (Frankenberg, 1993, p. 236). As such I wish to propose a model that may be less susceptible to dismissal by white people as being too located within individual frameworks.

A Different Model

I argue that white people as individuals are situated within a frame we can loosely call White Racial Identity (WRI). If understood as a single, yet complex, frame and less of a series of static constructs through which an individual works, we also understand that the framework has many attributes or characteristics that those within the frame can draw from and possess. The particular characteristics that live within the framework, and not in any one particular status, could be understood as attributes comprising one's white racial propriospect (WRP). Propriospect is a concept developed by Goodenough (1974) and later expanded by Wolcott (1983) to help balance distinction in culture between shared culture and individual representations of cultural elements drawn from the larger cultural group. In a sense, one's propriospect is the unique makeup of characteristics that draw from the larger structure that houses all cultural characteristics. In that sense one's WRP could then be understood as the particular and individual manifestations of WRI, while recognizing that WRP is not an individual in isolation but rather the individual within the larger structure of the WRI framework. Nesting WRP within WRI creates a back-and-forth motion that links individual white people to other white people. The back-and-forth orientation, from shared to individual, creates a larger ability to see one's individual manifestation of racial identity as both living inside her or him, while simultaneously existing in concert with other white people who draw characteristics from the same structured framework. To link the individual white person with other white people is part of Frankenberg's (1993) call to examine white supremacy, whiteness, and racism in more global and systemic ways.

In the Helms model, characteristics of white racial identity are restricted to and presented within particular statuses and again disconnected from a more connected way of knowing. In this new model of WRI, the characteristics that help to shape and form one's WRP could be considered as existing more systemically within the global structure of white racial identity. In other words, all the characteristics, behaviors, and aspects endemic to whiteness would be a sort of white racial manifest, a full complement of characteristics associated with our whiteness. With the whiteness manifest as part of the more global structure of white racial identity, individual white people within the structure of WRI possess particular characteristics from the manifest in varying degrees at varying times, and would represent the WRP as their individual inventory of characteristics. For me as a child, my WRI might be more marked by the characteristic of racial naïveté and, as an adult, the naïveté may take a less prominent position within my WRP, whereas the characteristic of color-blind language may take the more prominent position. I argue that once a characteristic from the manifest is present in the individual inventory, it never disappears or goes away from one's WRP, but rather shifts in terms of visibility and weight within the total understanding of one's WRP within the larger WRI frame. In the proposed model, WRI is fluid, and individual manifestations of propriospect are not restricted to movement through static statuses, but rather the WRP of each individual within the framework is continually and always evolving with characteristics shifting in weight to represent the growth and regression that is natural to the human experience. Moreover, in this model, the individual white racial propriospect would not be understood as being a singular unified element. Rather, an individual's propriospect would be understood as complex itself, and each of Johari's windows discussed earlier is present. The model changes the sense of identity from being that which one possesses as an individual to that of a more global structure that all white people possess and that frames whiteness. The model also adds a layer of complexity and nuance to understanding the propriospect of each individual within the White Racial Identity model, further distinguishing the model from Helms' conceptualization.

Differences in the Model

My approach in presenting WRI differs from Helms's approach in significant ways. First, I propose that a particular characteristic does not vanish when a more evolved appearing characteristic arrives in one's WRP. For example, Helms presents racial naïveté as being characteristic of the Contact Status but never discusses how racial naïveté is present in later statuses. In the study explored throughout this book only three of the ten participants appeared to be in the Contact Status as proposed by Helms (1990, 2003), yet racial naïveté is absolutely present in each of the participants' narratives and my own narrative. In the proposed model, racial naïveté would consequently be a part of each of our WRPs, an aspect of our propriospect of which we need to be consciously aware, as opposed to thinking we have moved beyond it. The degree to which the characteristic of racial naïveté is present in each participant's narrative differs, but for those of us who present as being "further along" in Helms's model, naïveté is still present. Moving toward understanding our WRP as part of WRI helps us understand that aspects of our propriospect will not leave simply because we also acquire other attributes from the manifest. In this model also, no one particular white person is ahead or behind another with respect to the construct of WRI; our propriospect is rather always in flux with the balance of constructs that are present. If the goal in developing one's understanding of WRI is to address issues of racial development that have gone unresolved, it is probably in the best interests of white people to engage with a model that recognizes that possessing what Helms presents as more evolved characteristics does not mean we break from characteristics that would be framed as more problematic or less evolved.

The second way in which the model differs is that WRI no longer becomes a discussion in isolation about individuals but rather recognizes that any individual white racial propriospect is always already situated within the larger framework of white supremacy. Participants in the model I propose have no set of statuses to pass through; rather, the WRI identity is seen as an organization to understand the ways in which white people collectively and individually work at maintaining our whiteness and its value, and how systematic racism and white supremacy work in concert with individuals and a whole system compromised of individuals. The focus in this new model becomes not an examination of individual identities but rather a construct in which an individual can understand both self and self as grouped. This distinction is important, particularly given the propensity of white denial and the ways that white people individually distance themselves from frameworks where constructs like racist, supremacist, judgmental, and so on, are present, as demonstrated by participants in this study.

For me the model involves shifting whiteness and white racial identity from the center that seeks to control those it relegates to the margins, to a balanced approach to humanity whereby whiteness can better interact within a structure at neither the center nor the margin of race, and in ways equitable for other races and other racial identities. As I will discuss in the last chapter, neither model can be effective unless white people are actively involved in the process of their white racial identity, and suggestions will be provided for how to utilize this expanded model of WRI.

Chapter 7
Implications and Future Directions

This book has attempted to conceptualize a new way of thinking about white racial identity, and WRI's impact, with the hopes of understanding how the narratives of the pre-service teachers might be used as means to better understand the enterprise of education in general, and to better understand the implications of white racial identity in particular. As presented earlier, this book and the related study are premised on three interrelated concepts: (1) the teaching force is comprised of up to 90% white teachers, (2) teachers are one of the primary socializers for children, and (3) the narratives of white pre-service teachers may prove helpful in understanding how white people understand their own whiteness. What emerges from studying the narratives of white pre-service teachers are discourse structures and patterns of participants' thinking across cases, which have helped to shape the overall framing of this work. In this concluding chapter, and as a means of reviewing the general scope of this book, I look at the implications of this research. To achieve this aim I both summarize the findings and present what I believe to be theoretical, pragmatic, and pedagogical implications of the work. I also share recommendations for other researchers based on lessons learned in doing this work. Finally I propose future directions for research.

Summary of Findings and Implications

Brief Summary of Findings

I provide a brief summary of the major ideas presented thus far in the book before delving into the implications of the work. Three categorical areas of ideas or themes provided the basis for the discussion in chapters 5, 6, and 7. The first theme in chapter 5 centered on how participants deployed particular semantic moves, namely, white racial bonding through discourse and color-blind-oriented discourse, as a means of discussing and negotiating the topic of race. The idea of color-blind discourse was further broken down to conceptualizations of abstract liberalism, naturalization, minimization, and confused or incoherent narratives about race. The second theme of the research in chapter 6 examined the uninformed and naïve articulations of why the pre-service teachers entered the profession of teaching, and I argued that the "naïve" rationales served as yet another semantic move related to race, in particular the demonstration of racial dysconsciousness. The third major theme of chapter 7 was a set of three interrelated ideas about white racial identity that suggested (1) participants' conceptualizations of white racial identity relegated issues of "race" to "diversity," (2) participants conceptualized their sense of white identity through racial others, and (3) participants exhibited a heightened sense of incoherence and confusion in conceptualizing their own white racial identity. With those ideas in mind I also located the participants within Helms's White Racial Identity Model, presented limitations of Helms's model, and argued for a new model that better situates individual white propriospect within the larger structure of white racial identity.

Implications and Recommendations

On the Rationales for Being Teachers

Given that the demographic landscape of the teaching force in the United States is comprised primarily of white teachers, an implication of this work relates to institutions of higher education charged with preparing educators. Participants' narratives illustrated the need for teacher preparation programs to problematize how pre-service teachers are admitted into programs, supported and pushed throughout their programs, monitored beyond their teacher education programs, and ultimately held accountable for their work as teachers. Part and parcel to such accountability is how pre-service teachers' racialized identities not only inform pedagogical choices but shape the socialization process by which children are influenced. To say there is much work to be done with the overwhelming whiteness in the teaching force would be an understatement. Whiteness, coupled with the candidates' inability to justify why they have chosen this profession, provides reason for pause in our preparation of educators. That the pre-service participants in this research could not articulate substantive or developed reasons and rationales for becoming teachers is alarming, yet, I argue, not unique to this participant pool; these ideas have held true upon further exploration with pre-service teachers at different institutions. I have worked as a teacher educator in several states and institutions, notably, in several pre-service teachers education programs in four states, and, while my experiences certainly may not provide sufficient evidence for a fully generalized claim, they do tell me that the narratives of the participants in this study are not unique (Fasching-Varner, 2009). In my interactions with pre-service teachers and educators, as well as in conversation with other teacher educators, the rationales that pre-service teachers articulate appear to be under-developed and rest greatly within cliché orientations of what it means to be a teacher.

Teaching is a complex endeavor, and even for folks who have well-articulated and substantive reasons for being a teacher, the work of being a culturally relevant, effective teacher is difficult (Ladson-Billings, 1994; Dixson & Fasching-Varner, 2008). The complexity and difficulty in preparing future teachers to deal with the realities of teaching, and the reality of the impact of teachers' racialized identities on students, are enhanced when the pre-service teachers themselves do not have significant rationales for entering the profession. I propose several steps to address the under-developed nature of pre-service teachers' rationales for becoming teachers.

First, teacher preparation programs need to be more conscious of the admissions process, use that process to intervene with prospective pre-service teachers, and help them develop a meaningful sense of why they have chosen the field; to that extent I call on pre-service teacher educators to begin directly involving the candidates in the process of articulating grounded and developed rationales for being teachers. Pre-service education programs need to have real conversations with potential teacher candidates during the admission process. Often complex checklists and admissions rubrics are used to make decisions on paper about people who "live" off of paper. Not only do such processes privilege students who are already privileged and have had better access to negotiating the structural systematic advantages of the system, but they also suggest that we often do not converse with potential applicants about why it is they are choosing this profession, and what their understandings of themselves are. At Righteous College, for example, much time was spent talking about teacher candidates and how to more robustly engage them, yet little time was actually spent talking with the teacher candidates to help them have a stake in this process, which may in fact help them develop more complex rationales for entering the profession.

In *Crossing over to Canaan*, Ladson-Billings (2001) highlighted how a program can think systematically about the candidates being admitted to the program so as to create the richest opportunity for teacher candidates to grow. Early in the process potential teacher candidates need to be asked about why they are entering the profession, and the narrative needs to be recorded by the candidate and then revisited throughout the program. This recorded rationale narrative becomes tangible and is a place the candidate can re-visit as she or he develops through the program. The recommendation is not to deny admission to anyone who does not exhibit a sufficiently developed rational for being a teacher, but rather to figure out where the teacher candidate is at that moment in time and what the program will need to think about in terms of experiences and opportunities to help the candidate develop wider angles of vision.

Programs should also create a set of stopping points at which candidates are required to re-examine the nature of their rationales and to continue developing their reasons for choosing this profession. These stopping points would allow candidates opportunities for self-reflection, and would also give programs a mechanism for examining the development of pre-service teacher candidates over time; this would provide teacher educators with fodder to develop themselves within the frameworks of our courses so that we can consciously address the nature of teaching within our courses. Also, a stopping point at the end of the program would allow program faculty to make informed choices about recommending candidates for certification or licensure. Often programs automatically recommend candidates for certification and/or licensure for simply completing the program.

It is often assumed that enduring and completing a program in teacher education and satisfying the higher educational institution requirements means that the teacher candidate will automatically be recommended for certification. In Lila's home state, teacher candidates cannot become certified or licensed to practice teaching without institutional recommendation. If candidates cannot substantively speak to and consciously identify why they are entering the profession by the end of their program, I suggest the program has a moral and ethical obligation to the candidate's future students to intervene and withhold the institutional recommendation. I believe clarity as to how candidates are recommended for licensure is a fundamental responsibility for potential students of candidates and for the communities at large that fund public education. This recommendation would require a less consumerist approach to how higher education operates, and an effort by institutions to be less concerned with lost revenue. Of course this would mean admitting committed candidates rather than everyone just to meet enrollment quotas, and preventing every candidate from moving to certification simply for enduring to the end. Not everyone who wants to be certified should be, particularly when candidates cannot demonstrate that they are prepared for the work. If teacher education programs graduate teacher candidates who are not ready to teach, school systems become further overburdened by teacher turnover and retention issues, and subsequently educational gaps in student achievement are likely to persist. Under-prepared teachers are likely to engage in poor pedagogy detrimental to student populations and, once they are tenured, they may become mentor teachers, socializing teacher candidates into the profession, a problematic training approach. The retention of strong, culturally relevant teachers begins not when teachers enter the profession in school districts, but rather it begins very early in the admittance process to teacher education programs.

On the Nature of Discourse

A significant idea developed throughout this book is that discourse is an important tool in understanding how people epistemologically conceptualize their worlds as revealed through their word (Lawrence, 1995, 2008), including the nature of beliefs about race. This book has presented findings related to participants' race discourse which are consistent with findings from other general studies of race (Bonilla-Silva, 2001, 2006). The nature of raced discourse of white people is fundamentally similar across settings and across participant samples. To that extent this book further contributes to the building base of our understanding of the nature of raced discourses. As addressed in the discussion, the nature of race discourse complements the work of CRT's focus on the property value of whiteness. This book makes a unique contribution to the literature in bringing the two concepts together, that is, the empirical examination of semantic moves articulated through participant discourse with the nature of CRT's discussion on whiteness property value.

By understanding semantic moves as demonstrative of an attempt to maintain whiteness' property value, the participants' narratives are placed not only within the singular frame of color-blind orientations, but also are indicators that color-blind discourse is a significant part of the larger hegemonic white supremacist structure that has been fundamentally part of the landscape in the United States (hooks, 2003). When understood in a frame beyond the individual participants themselves, and existing in the larger enterprise of maintaining whiteness which does not occur in isolation, there is less opportunity to claim that such semantic moves are not indicative of socialized and internalized racism. The focus of our understanding of individual white people within the system of whiteness cannot be reduced to simply who is "good/bad," "racist/non-racist," "nice/mean." In fact, I argue we are better served by creating a space to understand that white educators enjoy a large number of systematic advantages and privileges, and that our discourse is the very site where we might understand how those privileges are protected through the maintenance of whiteness' value. The propensity of the pre-service teachers studied was to situate themselves within frameworks of ideological openness to create semantic distance from those they conceptualized as racially problematic and unlike themselves. The need to distance oneself from supposedly racially problematic people is supported when we look at race through the lens of individual narrative. In such an orientation, all that a white person needs to do is create semantic distance, and voila! she or he is not racist. This book links race-embedded narrative with whiteness as property in an attempt to move thinking beyond the individualist approach toward understanding the maintenance of white privilege.

A problem in this thinking is that as researchers, we may be able to see the insight of the value to linking color-blind discourse with CRT elements, but pre-service teachers often do not have the opportunity in their teacher education program to see and situate themselves within the larger framework of race. Sierra was a discrepant case within the group of pre-service teachers in this book as she was beginning to understand her individual beliefs as existing within a structure of white racism, white supremacy, and the overall maintenance of whiteness' property value. The other participants still positioned themselves as rational and consequently non-racist, and I argue that while it is always ultimately the candidates' responsibility for movement toward anti-racism, it is pre-service teacher educators' responsibility to (1) model movement toward anti-racism, (2) create experiences that foster such movement, and (3) hold candidates responsible when sufficient movement has not occurred through a candidate's time in the pre-service teacher education program.

Pre-service teachers need their narratives made available to them in such a way that they too can engage in seeing their whiteness, demonstrated through their narratives and semantic moves. Once the narratives are available, they may be better positioned to understand theoretical constructs through the lens of their own narratives as they relate to difference, be it race, class, gender, or sexuality. One of the powerful forms of avoidance in teacher education programs is that candidates are able to circumvent themselves in the name of learning about others in order to do a better job. How do I teach _____? What are strategies to engage _____? In this orientation much of the pedagogical training becomes about others and filling in the blanks. Since most pre-service teacher candidates are white, they rarely have to examine their own racial identity and the implication of said identity in their pedagogical decisions. Early in their programs, teacher candidates should be given an interview protocol similar to the one used with the pre-service teachers in this study. To accomplish this, pre-service teachers should first be interviewed generically about their school and family experiences growing up, their rationales for becoming teachers, and their thoughts about teaching; then they should be given the opportunity to transcribe their own testimonial data. Following the transcription of the data, the pre-service teachers would be given a second interview protocol that revisited the same topics but through the lens of race; potentially the conversation would expand to include gender, class, sexuality, and so on. They would also transcribe the second interview, and the transcriptions would then become a tool that would be used to explore concepts that the candidates learn throughout their program, with the intent of reducing the level of abstractness and distance in understanding concepts like race. When talking about color-blind discourses, for example, teacher candidates would not be able to say, "Ohhh, I don't do that," but rather, with their instructors' guidance, would be able to see *how* they engage with race from color-blind perspectives, and perhaps be more willing to situate and see themselves within the system of whiteness that serves as a foundational base to their experiences.

On White Racial Identity

The final and perhaps most important ideas presented in this book relate to white racial identity—how white racial identity itself manifests through discourse structures. White racial identity has the potential to serve as yet another analytic layer in helping to understand the nature of whiteness in more profound ways. As a construct, my critique of Helms's White Racial Identity model indicates that the model may not effectively serve the purpose of helping white people understand the dual balance between themselves as individuals and the nature of being individuals within a group. Even if the model helped white people to see the situated nature of racial identity proposed in my new model of WRI, WRI is of limited utility if not actually in the hands of white people.

Given the nature of pre-service teacher training and professional interests in education, it is important that white pre-service teachers have opportunities to be presented with a model of WRI in concert with their own narratives, and which could be used for understanding themselves. Such a model could help pre-service teachers resist the temptation to view their training as an opportunity to learn about "others" or to further exploit minority populations in coming to terms with self. Given the recommendation for pre-service teachers' narratives to become a part of their own training, the use of the model of WRI presented in this book could be an effective tool for white pre-service teachers to examine themselves theoretically. For non-white pre-service teachers, I think the examination of their narratives and experiences would be interesting juxtaposed not only against the WRI model, but within the other models of identity development that are extant.

In using my model, participants would have to address the nature of their whiteness, and would have a theoretical language for doing so. A shortfall of the work in whiteness studies is that white researchers are apt to talk about other white people's whiteness without critical self-reflection. Consequently there is a necessity for white faculty to make public our own narratives, our own experiences, and our own struggles with our whiteness, and the examination of our whiteness within the structure of the global white supremacy. Whereas I suggest that white pre-service teachers need to examine their narratives and use a WRI model as a theoretical structure to understand their whiteness, so do the faculty who work with pre-service teachers. The most meaningful instantiation of this for me was the experience with Ana presented earlier. Prior to having Ana in my course, I was able to talk to pre-service teachers about the work they had to do, but always factored my own experiences out of the equation.

One of the most powerful dynamics in my teaching has become the opportunity for candidates to see me as vulnerable and in a position to do the same things I ask them to do. I say this again not to bring attention to me as doing something honorable or great, but just doing what is right and needed. I am white, and to not acknowledge my own whiteness, to leave it unexamined, or to not model a process for understanding the nature of whiteness, white supremacy, and white privilege, it would be impossible to help candidates do that same self-interrogation process. Ultimately the process of white faculty modeling how self-interrogation of our own experience can occur is also likely to reduce white students' need to use students and faculty of color as their learning experience, yet another toll of whiteness' destructive power against people of color.

Implications in Concert

It is important for us to consider the implications of the findings of this text in totality. In chapter 1, I framed this research with what Ladson-Billings (2006b) has highlighted as the educational debt with which students of color are burdened, a debt that is created by the historic, economic, socio-political, and moral debts created by white supremacist hegemony. My hope as an educator is to genuinely prepare teachers to better serve the needs of the children they teach, and to break the cycles of hegemony created by white people who have created the educational debts of which Ladson-Billings writes. Therefore, it is important to look at how the findings and implications of this research can work in tandem to help address the debt.

Part of the education debt comes from having teachers enter the teaching workforce unsure of the truth of why they have entered the field and full of dysconsciouss, yet ever-present beliefs and conceptualizations that prevent them from making authentic connections to their students, their students' families, and the communities where the families live. The teaching force is unlikely to change dramatically in a meaningful way; over the past thirty years the teaching force has been comprised of 85–92% white teachers. Pragmatically, we need more teachers of color and a richer tapestry of diverse teachers, a simple recommendation and implication of many research projects. Increasing teacher candidates of color is difficult given, for example, institutional resistance through gatekeeping practices that block students of color from admittance to undergraduate programs. Often students of color in pre-service teacher education programs are one of a few or may be the only student of color, and the pressures of being socialized to the profession surrounded and engulfed by whiteness is difficult to bear. Accepting more students of color into a program is meaningless without addressing the lack of critical consciousness that is the underpinning of pre-service teacher education programs.

The presence of students of color will not in and of itself change the orientation of white teachers, and white teachers will likely continue to compromise a significant portion of the teaching population. As a mathematical reality, we know that most new teachers will obtain employment in urban areas. Many of the pre-service teacher participants presented in this book wanted to teach in urban areas, and even for those who may have wished to teach in suburban areas, the jobs just are not there. Suburban teachers are retained longer than urban teachers and there is significantly less turnover, creating fewer open positions in suburban districts; our political geography dictates that as a sheer issue of number, more teaching positions will be available in urban districts as opposed to suburban or even rural districts.

Given these realities about teachers, the findings presented in this text, and the implications of these findings, the project of developing white teachers is necessary since it is likely that the teaching force generally will be composed of them, and it is likely that white teachers will continue teaching populations most affected by the education debt. Thus it is important to ensure that pre-service teachers do not simply become teachers by enduring their teacher preparation programs and without being able to substantiate the reasons they are entering the profession. Programs' moral and ethical responsibilities dictate paying better attention to the people whom institutions are recommending for state licensure or certification. Additionally, with more grounded and developed rationales, white teachers must leave their teacher education programs better aware of their whiteness, and more in touch with the individual and systemic manifestations of racialized beliefs, including racism and white supremacy, since there is likely to be a racial mismatch between them and the students they will teach. Through understanding the social and moral costs of our white supremacy, white racism, and the value we attach to our whiteness, teachers can better seek to service the principal of the debt created by the history of our racial identity.

Such understandings will also lessen the likelihood of negative racialized beliefs from adversely changing the types of pedagogical and educational opportunities offered to K–12 students. For those pre-service teachers who will teach in suburban settings with people they conceptualize as more like them, the work is equally important. In developing rationales for teaching and by understanding themselves as raced and beneficiaries of racism and white supremacy, they can begin to dismantle the comfortable socialization practices that currently teach white students what it means to be white. Regardless of teaching location, white educators as the historically and contemporarily privileged group have the responsibility for dismantling the walls of the house that racism built.

Future Directions for Researchers

In concluding this book I wish to leave readers with some thoughts about future directions for research. These thoughts are important to continue developing this field of study. A future direction for research must be the involvement of researchers in more longitudinal studies that work with pre-service teachers over time, from entering their program through their early career, through development, and through their pursuant teaching career. Long-term sustained research is difficult given people's movement and their life path changes; no longitudinal study has been undertaken, however, to understand the development of whiteness over a long term, as over the span of one's career in the public sector, and especially teaching. I argue that long-term longitudinal studies that begin with freshman undergraduates and follow them at least through the process of tenure are significantly important to fully understanding the nature of how racial identity factors into a teacher's career.

For white researchers who commit to writing about race and researching race with educators, I recommend examining the process of their own race, infusing auto-ethnographic elements with the study of race and pre-service teachers, so that the research can be understood as transformative; as researchers, we, too, are implicated in the work, and are not just researchers detached from our own lives and the ways in which our lives have derived from privileged white supremacist spaces.

Finally, it is imperative that more research to be conducted to examine the institutional orientations of teacher educator programs. The focus of this study was not on the pre-service teacher education program at Righteous College, but what emerged in this study is the need to better understand what it is that is actually being taught in pre-service teacher preparation programs, so that we can understand disconnects that surface in candidates' understandings of what they are learning. For example, how do we deal with the focus of this study, conversations of race, within pre-service teacher education programs? At Righteous College, candidates take one single disconnected course about issues related to race, class, gender, sexuality, and so on. The orientation of "diversity" is not intraprogramatic and this lends to disconnect for students. I believe that, by studying the workings of programs in teacher preparation, researchers can begin to understand the cross-sectional relationships between teacher candidates and the programs that educate them to the profession.

Afterword
The Long Hard Look

By Roland W. Mitchell

One of the most powerful lessons that I learned in my preparation to be a teacher was to be cognizant of just how little I actually know. And particularly, in instances where I find myself the most confident, or granted the greatest level of influence, it is vitally important that I remain suspect about my supposed understandings/expertise, and the subsequent actions that emerge from this place of confidence. I will go into greater detail about the nature of what I will call a "productive ignorance" shortly, but for now I believe that for teachers, this cautionary note about the depth of our knowing proffers a powerful lesson. The very act of becoming a teacher provides socialization that risks developing a chauvinism or teacher privilege (Mitchell & Edwards, 2010), in which educators are vested with unparalleled influence in their classrooms and in the lives of their students, while being simultaneously yoked with the weight of passing on hegemonic epistemologies, norms, and ultimately ways of living to the next generation.

I was provided a particularly poignant illustration of these ongoing lessons in humility by my major professor when I was completing my doctoral studies. Despite the fact that he was an alumnus of one of the most prestigious universities in the country, had studied with a world-renowned educator, and was in the process of earning a reputation as an emerging scholar himself, there was still one vitally important lesson that he believed himself to be ill-equipped to teach. His remarks about this lesson were, "I can teach you how to be a successful professor; I cannot teach you how to navigate a systemically racist university, however, as an African American professor."

Nearly a decade after completing my degree and serving as an advisor for numerous educators of varying racial and ethnic backgrounds, my advisor's comments have stuck with me. What I consider to be the truth associated with these remarks—race/racism has real consequences in students' lives—at that moment and still today comes as little surprise (West, 1990). As an African American, a member of a population that has faced the full brunt of state-sanctioned and de facto white supremacy, I did not need formal education, much less a graduate degree, to come to this conclusion. However, in a neo-liberal and tenaciously color-blind nation (Taubman, 2009; Marable & Mullings, 2000) with a requisite educational system (Anderson, 1988; Watkins, 2001; Apple, 1995) my advisor's recognition of the limitations of his knowledge as an individual in a privileged position within that system represented a space for much-needed inquiry. It is my opinion that this stance opens up the possibility for a productive type of ignorance. The opportunity for better understanding our roles as advisors to pre-service teachers, our relationship to disjointed and often conflicting knowledge communities, and subsequently our position in resisting/continuing existing epistemic violence enacted against particular segments of our student population, we are charged to "Primum non nocere," or "First, do no harm," as referenced in the foreword to this text by Adrienne Dixson.

Consequently, what I did find to be remarkable was the fact that my advisor, a European American man who from his prestigious education and middle-class American sensibilities to his current position at a leading university, could possess such clarity when considering these issues. Further, this clarity directly challenges pervasive narratives that circulate within teacher education programs that good teachers are all-knowing (intellectual chauvinism) and see all students as the same (color-blind). Subsequently, I see this type of critical reflexivity on the part of my advisor, his particular knowledge of self, and his recognition of his subject position within the dominant educational power structure as exceptional. However, given our uniquely American educational conundrum, where arguably the students in most need of dedicated teachers receive the poorest educational service (Ladson-Billings, 2006; Delpit & Dowdy, 2002; Dibble & Rosiek, 2002), my advisor's exceptionality troubles me.

The Implications of a Long Hard Look

It is my belief that my major professor's self-reflective perspective is crucial for white educators teaching racially diverse student populations. In fact, all educators, regardless of their racial identity, should be required to do the difficult work of first recognizing the role of formal schooling in privileging some communities and systemically disenfranchising others. And then they must perform the gut-wrenching and laborious task of looking inward to assess their "implicated-ness" in this disenfranchisement. Informed by these two exercises in self-discovery, novice teachers see their charge as much more complex than wanting to enter the profession "to help students," or because "I love kids." It may very well be the case that despite our sense of compassion or empathy, our inability to take a sober look in the mirror and arrive at a deeper purpose for teaching affords us the unintentional, yet no less damning, identity as a cog in the system of institutional disenfranchisement of students of color.

The point of this lengthy discussion of a moment in my own cross-cultural mentoring relationship was to provide an illustration of a white teacher who had arrived at a critical juncture in his responsibility as an educator. He was hyper-vigilant of his actions as a result of recognizing both the totality of educational oppression that students of color face as well as his location within that same system of oppression. Clearly, this particular case is anecdotal but there are numerous examples of white educators assuming a similar position in the literature from Scheurich's (2002) *Anti-racist Scholarship: An Advocacy* to Ignatiev and Garvey's (1996) *Race Traitor* and McIntosh's (1989) *White Privilege: Unpacking the Invisible Knapsack*. This perspective embodies what philosopher William James would describe as living a moral life, or for our purposes, teaching in a strenuous mood, as opposed to easily riding the rails of the dominant educational paradigm (James, 1897).

Within the current text, *Working Through Whiteness: Examining White Racial Identity and Profession with Pre-service Teachers*, Fasching-Varner provides a greatly needed addition to the literature of white scholars engaging against systemic racism. Where previous texts in varying ways document the impact of systemic white supremacy, illustrate the scope of the problem, or consider its effect on teachers and students, I believe still more is needed. Even my own anecdote concerning my major professor provides little more than a finished illustration of a white educator who has arrived at this thoughtful frame of mind for teaching in a racially diverse setting. But there remains the question, what did it take to get there? And while I do find these illustrations useful, for all intents and purposes, they amount to asking readers to construct a building without providing a blueprint. What Fasching-Varner gives white teacher educators, pre-service teachers, and educational administrators, however, is an actual working text, a how-to book, or blueprint of sorts, to start the arduous task of self-exploration keenly focused on how their racial identity development and sense of whiteness inform their pedagogical beliefs.

Further, as all good educators do, Fasching-Varner not only calls on pre-service teachers and their educators to do this self-reflexive work, but he models the behavior himself. Hence, throughout the text he tells his personal auto-ethnographic story of coming to terms with the ways race and racism caused him to relate to his students and teaching in general. Fasching-Varner demonstrates a level of intimate disclosure that is the antithesis to the position that systemic white supremacy affords white male teachers. As critical race theory asserts, one of the benefits of whiteness is the ability to resist the harsh realities associated with owning up to privileges associated with possessing whiteness as property (Yosso, 2005). Against the grain of racialized subjectivity, however,

Fasching-Varner actually, in a Freirean (1970) sense, illustrates that an essential part of countering the dehumanizing effects of white supremacy on white folks is staunchly connected to doing the heart-work of attempting to divest from the wages of whiteness.

Therefore, as readers move forward from this text, I have specific points that I would like for teacher educators and pre-service teachers to ponder. First and foremost Fasching-Varner's ideas have caused me to see that establishing dialogical and reciprocal relationships among schools and historically marginalized communities is vital for dismantling the racially oppressive aspects of our current educational system. However, these relationships must not be hermeneutically sealed. By this I mean as educators we must be vigilant about our constantly renegotiated positions as teachers and students in pedagogical spaces. Just as we teach, we need to be willing to be taught. And these lessons will sometimes be led by our students, parents, and community members as they concern aspects of their individual and group experiences that are a result of being socialized within a racist society and may be harder for white educators to perceive. As we do this work, the lingering possibility of our ignorance and/or the depth of our lack of understanding should not be shunned—recall this is a productive type of ignorance. And consequently we must be opened and actively seek out opportunities to fill this space with diverse and more profound understandings that reside in the blind spots outside the dominant schooling culture.

Accordingly, we should not avoid difference or see our role as teachers to be an ongoing search for a unified way of understanding the complexities of twenty-first century living. Further, the issues forwarded by Fasching-Varner in this book dampen the seemingly optimistic and extremely idealistic narratives provided by pre-service teachers. Consequently, the text reflects the wide chasm of experience between the current predominantly white, female, and middle-class teacher population and the increasingly racially, culturally, and ethnically diverse student population. This difference does not necessarily represent conflict. It does mean, however, that teachers are challenged to build relationships with their students in vastly different ways than those being forwarded by the bulk of existing teacher education programs. And consequently, as Fasching-Varner suggests, being in relation concerns knowing your students, but most importantly for white teachers, this actually means better understanding yourselves.

References

Anderson, J. (1988). *The education of blacks in the south 1860–1935*. Chapel Hill and London: University of North Carolina Press.

Apple, M. (1995). *Education and power*. New York, NY: Routledge.

Delpit, L., & Dowdy, J. (2002). *The skin that we speak: Thoughts on language and culture in the classroom*. New York, NY: New Press.

Dibble, N., & Rosiek, J. (2002). White-out: A connection between a teacher's white identity and her science teaching. *International Journal of Education and the Arts, 5*(3).

Freire, P. (1970). *Pedagogy of the oppressed.* New York & London: Continuum International Publishing Group.

Garvey, J., & Ignatiev, I. (1996). *Race traitor.* New York, NY: Routledge.

James, W. (1956). The will to believe and other essays in popular philosophy, 1897. Reprinted in *Human immortality: Two supposed objections to the doctrine,* New York, NY: Dover Publications, 1956.

Ladson-Billings, G.J. (2006). From achievement gap to education debt. Presidential Keynote Address, American Education Research Association. San Francisco, CA.

Marable, M., & Mullings, L. (2000). *Let nobody turn us around: Voices of resistance, reform, and renewal.* Boston, MA: Rowman & Littlefield Publishers.

McIntosh, P. (1989). White privilege: Unpacking the invisible knapsack. *Peace and Freedom,* 10–12.

Mitchell, R., & Edwards, K. (2010). Power, privilege, and pedagogy: College classrooms as sites to learn racial equity. In T. Elon Dancy (Ed.), *Managing diversity: (Re)visioning equity on college campuses.* (pp.45–68). Charlotte, NC: Information Age Press.

Rosiek, J. (2003). Emotional scaffolding: An exploration of teacher knowledge at the intersection of student emotion and subject matter content. *The Journal of Teacher Education, 54*(5), 399–412.

Scheurich, J. (2002). *Anti-racist scholarship: An advocacy.* New York, NY: State University of New York Press.

Taubman, P. (2009). *Teaching by numbers: Deconstructing the discourse of standards and accountability in education.* New York, NY: Routledge.

Watkins, W. (2001). *The white architects of black education: Ideology and power in America, 1865–1954.* New York, NY: Teachers College Press.

West, C. (1990). *Race matters.* Boston, MA: Beacon Press.

Yosso, T. J. (2005). Whose culture has capital? A critical race theory discussion of community cultural wealth. *Race, Ethnicity & Education, 8*(1), 69–91.

Bibliography

Adams, A., Bondy, E., & Kuhel, K. (2005). Preservice teacher learning in an unfamiliar setting. *Teacher Education Quarterly, 32*(2), 41–62.

Akbar, N. L. (1974). African roots of Black personality. In W. Smith, K. Burlew, M. Mosley, & W. Whitney (Eds.), *Reflections on Black psychology* (pp. 79–87). Washington, DC: University Press of America.

Applebaum, B. (2007). White complicity and social justice education: Can one be culpable without being liable? *Educational Theory, 57,* 453–467.

Asher, N. (2007). Made in the (multicultural) UNITED STATESA.: Unpacking tensions of race, culture, gender, and sexuality in education. *Educational Researcher, 36*(2), 65–73.

Associated Press. (2003, January 13). White teachers fleeing black schools. Retrieved September 12, 2008.

Ball, A. F. (2002). Three decades of research on classroom life: Illuminating the classroom communicative lies of America's at-risk students. *Review of Research in Education, 26,* 71–111.

Banks, J. A. (1981). The stages of ethnicity: Implications for curriculum reform. In J. A. Banks (Ed.), *Multi-ethnic education: Theory and practice* (pp. 129–139). Boston, MA: Allyn & Bacon.

Bell, D. (1995a*). Brown v. Board of Education* and the interest convergence dilemma. In K. Crenshaw, N. Gotanda, G. Peller, & K. Thomas (Eds.) *Critical race theory: The key writings that formed the movement* (pp. 20–28). New York, NY: New Press.

Bell, D. (1995b). Racial Realism. In K. Crenshaw, N. Gotanda, G. Peller, & K. Thomas (Eds.), *Critical race theory: The key writings that formed the movement* (pp. 302–314). New York, NY: New Press.

Bonilla-Silva, E. (2001). *White supremacy and racism in the post–civil rights era.* London, UK: Lynne Rienner Publishers.

Bonilla-Silva, E. (2003). *Racism without racists: Color-blind racism and the persistence of racial inequality in the United States* (1st ed.). New York, NY: Rowman & Littlefield Publishers.

Bonilla-Silva, E. (2006). *Racism without racists: Color-blind racism and the persistence of racial inequality in the United States* (2nd ed.). Lanham, MD: Rowman & Littlefield Publishers.

Brearley, H. C. (1947). The preeminence of the teacher. *Peabody Journal of Education, 25*(2), 75–78.

Brooks, W., Browne, S., & Hampton, G. (2008). "There ain't no accounting for what folks see in their own mirrors": Considering colorism with a Sharon Flake narrative. *Journal of Adolescent & Adult Literacy, 51,* 660–669.

Brown v. Board of Education of Topeka, 347 UNITED STATES 483 (1954).

Brown, M. K., Carnoy, M., Currie, E., Duster, T., Oppenheimer, D. B., Shultz, M. M., & Wellman, D. (2003). *Whitewashing race: The myth of a color-blind society.* Riverside, CA: University of California Press.

Brown, P., & Levinson S. (1987). *Politeness: Some universals in language usage.* Cambridge, UK: Cambridge University Press.

Caliver, A. (1936). The role of the teacher in the reorganization and redirection of Negro education. *The Journal of Negro Education, 5*(3), 508–516.

Carter, R. T., & Goodwin, A. L. (1994). Race identity and education. *Review of Research in Education, 20,* 291–336.

Carter, R. T., & Helms, J. E. (1988). The relationship between racial identity attitudes and social class. *The Journal of Negro Education, 57*(1), 22–30.

Carter, R. T., Helms, J. E., & Juby, H. I. (2004). The relationship between racism and racial identity for white Americans: A profile analysis. *Journal of Multicultural Counseling and Development, 31*(1), 2–17.

Catalogna, L., Greene, J. F., & Zirkel, P. A. (1981). An exploratory examination of teachers' perceptions of pupils' race. *The Journal of Negro Education, 50,* 370–380.

Chubbuck, S. M. (2004). Whiteness enacted, whiteness disrupted: The complexity of personal congruence. *American Educational Research Journal, 41*(2), 301–333.

Clandinin, D. J., & Connelly, F. M. (2004). *Narrative inquiry: Experience and story in qualitative research.* San Francisco, CA: Jossey-Bass.

Clark, C., & O'Donnell, J. (1999). *Becoming and unbecoming white: Owning and disowning a racial identity.* Santa Barbara, CA: Praeger Press.

Cochran-Smith, M. (2000). Blind vision: Unlearning racism in teacher education. *Harvard Educational Review, 70,* 157–190.

Compton-Lilly, C. (2000). "Staying on children": Challenging stereotypes about urban parents. *Language Arts, 77*(5), 420–427.

Compton-Lilly, C. (2003). *Reading families: The literate lives of urban children.* New York, NY: Teachers College Press.

Compton-Lilly, C. (2004). *Confronting racism, poverty, and power: Classroom strategies to change the world.* Portsmouth, NH: Heinemann.

Compton-Lilly, C. (2005a). "Sounding out": A pervasive cultural model of reading. *Language Arts, 82,* 441–451.

Compton-Lilly, C. (2005b). Nuances of Error: Considerations relevant to African American Vernacular English and learning to read. *Literacy, Teaching, and Learning, 10*(1), 43–58.

Compton-Lilly, C. (2006). Identity, childhood culture, and literacy learning: A case study. *Journal of Early Childhood Literacy, 6*(1), 57–76.

Compton-Lilly, C. (2007a). Exploring reading capital in two Puerto Rican families. *Reading Research Quarterly, 42*(1), 72–98.

Compton-Lilly, C. (2007b). *Rereading families: The literate lives of urban children, the intermediate years.* New York, NY: Teachers College Press.

Cook-Gumperz, J. (1993). Dilemmas of identity: Oral and written literacies in the making of a basic writing student. *Anthropology and Education Quarterly, 24*, 336–356.

Copenhaver-Johnson, J. (2006). Talking to children about race: The importance of inviting difficult conversations. *Childhood Education, 83*(1), 12–22.

Crenshaw, K. W. (1995). Race, reform, and retrenchment: Transformation and legitimation in anti-discrimination law. In K. Crenshaw, N. Gotanda, G. Peller, & K. Thomas (Eds.), *Critical race theory: The key writings that formed the movement* (pp. 103–126). New York, NY: New Press.

Cross, W. E., Jr. (1971). The Negro-to-Black conversion experience: Toward a psychology of Black liberation. *Black World, 20*(9), 13–27.

Cross, W. E., Jr. (1978). Models of psychological nigrescence: A literature review. *Journal of Black Psychology, 5*(1), 13–31.

Cross, J. B., DeVaney, T., & Jones, G. (2001). Pre-service teacher attitudes toward differing dialects. *Linguistics and Education, 12*, 211–227.

Cross, W. E., Jr., Paraham, T. A., & Helms, J. E. (1991). Nigrescence revisited: Theory and research. In R. L. Jones (Ed.), *African American Identity Development: Advances in Black psychology*. Berkeley, CA: Cobb & Henry.

DeCuir, J. T., & Dixson, A. D. (2004). "So when it comes out, they aren't surprised it is there": Using critical race theory as a tool of analysis of race and racism in education. *Educational Researcher*, 26–31.

DeCuir-Gunby, J. T. (2006). "Proving your skin is white, you can have everything": Race, racial identity, and property rights in whiteness in the supreme court case of Josephine DeCuir. In. A. Dixson & C. Rousseau (Eds.), *Critical race theory in education: All God's children got a song* (pp. 89–112). New York, NY: Routledge.

Delgado, R. (1989). Storytelling for oppositionists and others: A plea for narrative. *Michigan Law Review, 87*, 2411–2441.

Delgado, R. (1990). When a story is just a story, does voice really matter? *Virginia Law Review, 76*, 95–111.

Delgado, R. (1993). On telling stories in school: A response to Farber and Sherry. *Virginia Law Review, 79*, 665–675.

Delgado, R., & Stefacnic, J. (1997). *Critical white studies: Looking behind the mirror*. Philadelphia, PA: Temple University Press.

Delgado, R., & Stefancic, J. (2001). *Critical race theory: An introduction*. New York, NY: New York University Press.

Delgado Bernal, D., & Villapando, O. (2002). An apartheid of knowledge in academia: The struggle over the "legitimate" knowledge of faculty of color. *Equity and Excellence in Education, 35*, 169–180.

Denzin, N. K. (1989). *The research act: A theoretical introduction to sociological methods* (3rd ed.). Englewood Cliffs, NJ: Prentice Hall.

Denzin, N. K., & Lincoln, Y. S. (2000). The discipline and practice of qualitative research. In N. K. Denzin & Y. S. Lincoln's (Eds.), *Handbook of qualitative research* (2nd ed.) (pp. 1–36). Thousand Oaks, CA: Sage

Denzin, N. K., & Lincoln, Y. S. (2003a). The discipline and practice of qualitative research. In N. K. Denzin & Y. S. Lincoln (Eds.) *The landscape of
qualitative research* (2nd ed.) (pp.1–46). Thousand Oaks, CA: Sage

Denzin, N. K., & Lincoln, Y. S. (2003b). Paradigms and perspectives in transition. In N. K. Denzin & Y. S. Lincoln (Eds.), *The landscape of qualitative
research* (2nd ed.) (pp. 245–252). Thousand Oaks, CA: Sage.

Denzin, N. K., & Lincoln, Y. S. (2003c). The seventh moment: Out of the past.
In N. K. Denzin & Y. S. Lincoln (Eds.), *The landscape of qualitative research* (2nd ed.) (pp. 611– 640). Thousand Oaks, CA: Sage

Dixson, A. D. (2005). Extending the metaphor: Notions of jazz in portraiture.
Qualitative Inquiry, 11(1), 106–137.

Dixson, A. D., & Rousseau, C. K. (2005). And we are still not saved: Critical
race theory in education ten years later. *Race, Ethnicity, and Education,
8*(1), 7–27.

Dixson, A. D., & Fasching-Varner, K. J. (2008). This is how we do it: Helping
teachers understand Culturally Relevant Pedagogy in diverse classrooms. In
C. Compton-Lilly (Ed.), *Breaking the silence: Recognizing the social and
cultural resources students bring to the classroom* (pp. 109–124). Newark,
DE: International Reading Association.

Dizzard, J. E. (1971). Black identity, social class, and Black power. *Journal of
Social Issues, 26*(1), 195–207.

Duncan, G. A. (2006). Critical race ethnography in education: Narrative, inequality, and the problem of epistemology. In. A. Dixson & C. Rousseau
(Eds.), *Critical race theory in education: All God's children got a song* (pp.
191–212). New York, NY: Routledge.

Duranti, A. (2007). Transcripts: like shadows on a wall. *Mind, Culture, and Ac-
tivity, 13*, 301–310.

Ellis, C., & Bochner, A. P. (1996). *Composing ethnography: Alternative forms
of qualitative writing.* Walnut Creek, CA: Alta Mira.

Eliasoph, N. (1997). "Close to home": The work of avoiding politics. *Theory
and Society, 26*, 605–647.

Erikson, E. H. (1963). *Youth: Change and challenge.* New York, NY: Basic
Books.

Erikson, E. H. (1968). *Identity: Youth and crisis.* New York, NY: Norton.

Fasching-Varner, K. J. (2006). Pedagogy of respect: The intergenerational influence of Black women's pedagogy of respect. *Midwestern Educational Researcher, 19*(2), 28–35.

Fasching–Varner, K. J. (2009). No! The team ain't alright: The individual and
institutional problematic of race. *Social Identities, 15*.

Fasching-Varner, K. J., Dodo Seriki, V. (2012). Moving beyond seeing with our
eyes wide shut. *Democracy and Education, 20*(1), Article 5.

Feagin, J. & Vera, H. (1995). *White racism: The basics.* New York, NY: Routledge.

Feistritzer, E., & Haar, C. K. (2005). Profile of teachers in the U.S. 2005. *National Center for Education Information.*

Ferber, A. L. (2003). Defending the culture of privilege. In M. S. Kimmel & A. L. Ferber (Eds.), *Privilege: A reader* (pp. 319–330). Boulder, CO: Westview.

Fine, M. (1997). Witnessing whiteness. In M. Fine, L. Powell, L. Weiss, & L. M. Wong (Eds.), *Off white: Readings on race, power, and society* (pp. 57–65). New York, NY: Routledge.

Frank, G. (1995). Life histories in occupational therapy clinical practice. *American Journal of Occupational Therapy, 50,* 251–264.

Frankenberg, R. (1993). *The social construction of whiteness: White women, race matters.* Minneapolis, MN: University of Minnesota Press.

Frankenberg, R. (1996a). When we are capable of stopping, we begin to see: Being white, seeing whiteness. In B. Thompson & S. Tyagi (Eds.), *Names we call home: Autobiography on racial identity* (pp. 3–18). New York, NY: Routledge.

Frankenberg, R. (1996b). Whiteness as an "unmarked" cultural category. In K. E. Rosenblum & T. C. Travis (Eds.), *The meaning of difference: American constructions of race, sex and gender, social class, and sexual orientation* (pp. 62–68). St. Louis, MO: McGraw-Hill Companies.

Frankenberg, R. (1997). *Displacing whiteness: Essays in social and cultural criticism.* Durham, NC: Duke University Press.

Frankenberg, R. (1999). Introduction: Local whiteness, localizing whitenesses. In R. Frankenberg (Ed.), *Displacing whiteness: Essays in social and cultural criticism* (pp. 1–34). Durham, NC: Duke University Press.

Frankenberg, R. (2001). The mirage of an unmarked whiteness. In B. B. Rasmussen, E. Klinenberg, I. J. Nexica, & M. Wary (Eds.), *The making and unmaking of whiteness* (pp. 72–96). Durham, NC: Duke University Press.

Frankenberg, R. (2005). *The social construction of whiteness: White women, race matters.* Minneapolis, MN: University of Minnesota Press.

Fry, R. (2007). *A changing racial and ethnic mix in United States public schools: White students are less isolated but Black people and Hispanics are more so.* Washington, DC: Pew Research Center.

Gaertner, S. L. (1976). Nonreative measures in racial attitude research: A focus on "liberals." In P. A. Katz's (Ed.), *Towards the elimination of racism* (pp.183–311). New York, NY: Pergamon Press.

Ganter, G. (1977). The socio-conditions of the white practitioner: New perspectives. *Journal of Contemporary Psychotherapy, 9*(1), 26–32.

Gay, G. (1984). Implications of selected models of ethic identity development for educators. *The Journal of Negro Education, 54*(1), 43–52.

Gay, G., & Kirkland, K. (2003). Developing cultural critical consciousness and self-reflection in preservice teacher education. *Theory Into Practice, 42*, 181–187.

Gee, J. P. (2001). Identity as an analytic lens for research in education. *Review of Research in Education, 25*, 99–125.

Geertz, C. (1977). *The interpretation of cultures: Selected essays.* New York, NY: Basic Books.

Giroux, H. A. (1997). Rewriting the discourse of racial identity: Towards a pedagogy and politics of whiteness. *Harvard Educational Review, 67*, 285–320.

Goodenough, W. (1974). Toward an anthropologically useful definition of religion. In A. E. Eister (Ed.), *Changing perspectives in the scientific study of religion* (pp. 165–184). New York, NY: Wiley.

Gordon, J. (2005). Inadvertent complicity: Color-blindness in teacher education. *Educational Studies, 38*, 135–153.

Grayson, S. M. (2000). *Symbolizing the past: Reading* Sankofa, Daughters of the Dust, & Eve's Bayou *as histories.* Lanham, MD: University Press of America.

Gumperz, J. J. (1972) The speech community. In P. P. Giglioli (Ed.), *Language and social context* (pp. 43–52). London, UK: Harmondsworth Penguin.

Hall, S. (1997). *Representation: Cultural representations and signifying practices.* Thousand Oaks, CA: Sage.

Hallman, H. I. (2007). Negotiating teacher identity: Exploring the use of electronic teaching portfolios with preservice English teachers. *Journal of Adolescent & Adult Literacy, 50*, 474–485.

Harris, C. I. (1995). Whiteness as property. In K. Crenshaw, N. Gotanda, G. Peller, & K. Thomas (Eds.), *Critical race theory: The key writings that formed the movement* (pp. 276–291). New York, NY: New Press.

Hartigan, J. J. (1999). Establishing the fact of whiteness. In R. D. Torres, L. F. Mirón, & J. X. Inda (Eds.) *Race, identity, and citizenship* (pp. 183–199). Malden, MA: Blackwell Publishing.

Haviland, V. S. (2008). Things get glossed over: Rearticulating the silencing power of whiteness in education. *Journal of Teacher Education 59*(1), 40–42.

Helms, J. E. (1984). Toward a theoretical explanation of the effects of race on counseling: A black and white mode. *Counseling Psychologist, 12*, 153–165.

Helms, J. E. (1990). *Black and white racial identity: Theory, research, and practice.* Westport, CT: Greenwood Press.

Helms, J. E. (1992a). *A race is a nice thing to have: A guide to being a white person or understanding the white people in your life.* Topeka, KS: Content Communications.

Helms, J. E. (1992b). The conceptualization of racial identity and other "racial" constructs. In E. J. Trickett, R. J. Watts, & D. Birman (Eds.), *Human diversity: Perspectives on people in context* (pp. 285–312). San Francisco, CA: Jossey-Bass.

Helms, J. E. (1993). I also said, "White racial identity influences white researchers." *Counseling Psychologist, 21*, 240–243.

Helms, J. E. (1994). Racial identity in the social environment. In P. Pederson & J. Carey (Eds.), *Multicultural counseling in schools: A practical handbook* (pp. 19–37). Boston, MA: Allyn & Bacon.

Helms, J. E. (1995). An update of Helms's white and people of color racial identity models. In J. G. Ponterotto, J. M. Casas, L. A. Suzuki, & C. M. Alexander (Eds.), *Handbook of multicultural counseling* (pp. 181–191). Thousand Oaks, CA: Sage.

Helms, J. E. (1997). Implications of Behrens (1997) for the validation of the white racial identity attitude scale. *Journal of Counseling Psychologist, 44*, 13–16.

Helms, J. E. (2003). A pragmatic view of social justice. *Counseling Psychologist, 31*, 305–313.

Hernandez Sheets, R. (2001). Whiteness and white identity in multicultural education. *Multicultural Education, 8*(3), 38–40.

Hill, M. (1997). *Whiteness: A critical reader.* New York, NY: New York University Press.

Hitchcock, J. (2002). *Lifting the white veil.* Roselle, NJ: Crandall, Dostie, & Douglass Books.

Hodder, I. (2003). The interpretation of documents and material culture. In N. K. Denzin & Y. S. Lincoln (Eds.), *Collecting and interpreting qualitative materials* (2nd ed.) (pp. 155–175). Thousand Oaks, CA: Sage.

hooks, b. (2000). *Feminist theory: From margin to center.* Boston, MA: South End Press.

hooks, b. (2003). Overcoming white supremacy. In L. Heldke & P. O'Connor (Eds.), *Oppression, privilege, and resistance,* (pp. 69–75). New York, NY: McGraw-Hill.

Howard, J. A. (2000). Social psychology of identities. *Annual Review of Sociology, 26*, 367–393.

Hurtado, A. (1999). The trickster's play: Whiteness in the subordination and liberation process. In R. D. Torres, L. F. Mirón, & J. X. Inda (Eds.), *Race, Identity, and Citizenship* (pp. 225–244). Malden, MA: Blackwell Publishing.

Ignatiev, N. (1995). *How the Irish became white.* New York, NY: Routledge.

Ignatiev, N. (1997a). Treason to whiteness is loyalty to humanity. In R. Delgado & J. Stefacnic (Eds.), *Critical white studies: Looking behind the mirror,* (pp. 607–612). Philadelphia, PA: Temple University Press.

Ignatiev, N. (1997b). How to be a race traitor: Six ways to fight being white. In
    R. Delgado & J. Stefancic (Eds.), *Critical white studies: Looking behind the
    mirror* (p. 629). Philadelphia, PA: Temple University Press.
Johnson, L. (2002). "My eyes have been opened": White teachers and racial
    awareness. *Journal of Teacher Education, 53,* 153–167.
Jones, J. M. (1972). *Prejudice and racism.* Reading, MA: Addison-Wesley Pub-
    lishers.
Jones, S. H. (2006). Auto-ethnography: Making the personal political. In N.
    Denzin & Y. Lincoln (Eds.), *The Sage handbook of qualitative research*
    (3rd ed.) (pp.763–791).
Kovel, J. (1970). *White racism: A psychohistory.* New York, NY: Pantheon.
Krieger, S. (1996). *The family silver: Essays on relationships among women.*
    Berkeley, CA: University of California Press.
Ladson-Billings, G. J. (1994). *The dreamkeepers: Successful teachers of African
    American children.* San Francisco, CA: Jossey-Bass.
Ladson-Billings, G. J. (2001). *Crossing over to Canaan: The journey of new
    teachers in diverse classrooms.* San Francisco, CA: Jossey-Bass.
Ladson-Billings, G. J. (2005). The evolving role of critical race theory in educa-
    tional scholarship. *Race, Ethnicity, and Education,* 8(1), 115–119.
Ladson-Billings, G. J. (2006a). "Your blues ain't like mine": Keeping issues of
    race and racism on the multicultural agenda. *Theory Into Practice, 35,* 248–
    255.
Ladson-Billings, G. J. (2006b). From achievement gap to education debt. Presi-
    dential keynote address, presented at the meeting of the American Educa-
    tion Research Association, San Francisco, CA.
Ladson-Billings, G. J., & Tate, W. F., IV. (1995). Toward a critical race theory
    of education. *Teachers College Record,* 97(1), 47–68.
Lather, P. (1986). Research as praxis. *Harvard Educational Review, 56,* 179–
    199.
Lawrence, C. R., III. (1995). The id, the ego, and equal protection: Reckoning
    with unconscious racism. In K. Crenshaw, N. Gotanga, G. Peller, K. Thom-
    as (Eds.), *Critical race theory: The key writings that formed the movement*
    (pp. 235–256). New York, NY: New Press.
Lawrence, C. R., III. (2008). Unconscious racism revisited: Reflections on the
    impact and origins of the id, the ego, and equal protection. *Connecticut Law
    Review, 40,* 1025–1033.
Lawrence, S. M., & Tatum, B. D. (1997). Teachers in transition: The impact of
    antiracist professional development on classroom practice. *Teachers Col-
    lege Record,* 99(1), 162–178.
Lee, S., & Dallman, M. E. (2008). Engaging in a reflective examination about
    diversity: Interviews with three preservice teachers. *Multicultural Educa-
    tion, 15*(4), 33–44.
Lensmire, T. J. (2008) How I became white while punching tar baby. *Curricu-
    lum Inquiry, 38*(3), 299-322.

Leonard, D. J. (2004). The next M. J. or the next O. J.? Kobe Bryant, race, and the absurdity of colorblind rhetoric. *Journal of Sport and Social Issues, 28,* 284–313.

Leonardo, Z. (2002). The souls of white folk: Critical pedagogy, whiteness studies, and globalization discourse. *Race, Ethnicity, and Education, 5*(1), 29–50.

Levine-Rasky, C. (1998). Preservice teacher education and the negotiation of social difference. *British Journal of Sociology in Education, 19*(1), 89–112.

Lincoln, Y. S., & Guba, E. (1985). *Naturalistic inquiry.* Thousand Oaks, CA: Sage.

Lincoln, Y. S., & Guba, E. G. (1989). Let whoever is without dogma cast the first stone. *Educational Researcher, 18*(2), 22.

Lipsitz, G. (1998). *The possessive investment in whiteness: How white people benefit from identity politics.* Philadelphia, PA: Temple University Press.

Lipsitz, G. (2005). Whiteness and war. In C. McCarthy, W. Crichlow, G. Dimitriadis, & N. Dolby (Eds.), *Race, identity, and representation in education* (pp. 95–115). New York, NY: Routlege Falmer.

Lipsitz, G. (2006). *The possessive investment in whiteness: How white people profit from identity politics.* Philadelphia, PA: Temple University Press.

Little, K. (1993). Masochism, spectacle, and the "broken mirror" clown entree: A note on anthropology of performance in postmodern culture. *Ethnographies of Technology, 8*(1), 117–129.

López, I. H. (2006). *White by law: The legal construction of race.* New York, NY: New York University Press.

Lowery, L. (1983). Bridging a culture in counseling. *Journal of Applied Rehabilitation Counseling, 14*(1), 69–73.

Luft J., & Ingham, H. (1955). *The Johari window: A graphic model of interpersonal awareness.* Los Angeles, CA: University of California Western Training Lab.

Marx, S., & Pennington, J. (2003). Pedagogies of critical race theory: Experimentations with white preservice teachers. *Qualitative Studies in Education, 16*(1), 91–110.

McAllister, G., & Irvine, J. J. (2000). Cross cultural competency and multicultural teacher education. *Review of Educational Research, 70*(1), 3–24.

McDermott, M. (2002). Collaging pre-service teacher identity. *Teacher Education Quarterly, 29*(4), 53–68.

McDermott, M., & Samson, F. L. (2005). White racial and ethnic identity in the United States. *Annual Review of Sociology, 31,* 245–261.

McIntosh, P. (1989, July/August). White privilege: Unpacking the invisible knapsack. *Peace and Freedom,* 10–12.

McIntyre, A. (2002). Exploring whiteness and multicultural education with prospective teachers. *Curriculum Inquiry, 32*(1), 31–38.

McWhorter, L. (2005). Where do white people come from: A Foucaultian critique of whiteness studies. *Philosophy & Social Criticism, 31,* 533–556.

Merseth, K. K., Sommer, J., & Dickstein, S. (2008). Bridging worlds: Changes in personal and professional identities of pre-service urban teachers. *Teacher Education Quarterly, 3*, 89–108.

Mills, C. W. (1997). *The racial contract.* Ithaca, NY: Cornell University Press.

Montague, A. (1997). *Man's most dangerous myth: The fallacy of race.* Walnut Creek, CA: Altamira.

Montecinos, C., & Nielson, L. E. (2004). Male elementary preservice teachers' gendering of teaching. *Multicultural Perspectives, 6*(2), 3–9.

Morrison, T. (1992). *Playing in the dark: Whiteness and the literary imagination.* New York NY. Vintage Books.

Newman, D. M. (2007). *Identities & inequalities: Exploring the intersections of race, class, gender, and sexuality.* New York, NY: McGraw-Hill.

Nudd, D. M., Schriver, K., & Galloway, T. (2001). Is this theater queer? The Micke Faust club and the performance community. In S. C. Haedick & T. Nelhaus (Eds.), *Performing democracy: International perspectives on urban community-based performance* (pp. 104–116). Ann Arbor, MI: University of Michigan Press.

Parker, L., & Lynn, M. (2002). What's race go to do with it?: Critical race theory's conflicts with and connections to qualitative research methodology and epistemology. *Qualitative Inquiry, 8*(1), 7–22.

Parsons, E. C. (2001). Using power and caring to mediate white male privilege, equality, and equity in an urban elementary classroom. *Urban Review, 33*, 321–338.

Patton, M. (1990). *Qualitative evaluation and research methods* (2nd ed.). Thousand Oaks, CA: Sage.

Peshkin, A. (1988). In search of subjectivity—One's own. *Educational Researcher, 17*(7), 17–21.

Philipsen, D. (2003). Investment, obsession, and denial: The ideology of race in the American mind. *Journal of Negro Education, 72*, 193–207.

Pollock, M. (2001). How the question we ask most about race in education is the very question we most suppress. *Educational Researcher, 30*(9), 2–12.

Ponterotto, J. G. (1989). Expanding directions for racial identity research. *Counseling Psychologist, 17*, 264–272.

Reason, R. D. (2007). Rearticulating whiteness: A precursor to difficult dialogues on race. *College Student Affairs Journal, 26*, 127–135.

Reed-Danahay, D. E. (1997). *Auto/ethnography: Rewriting the self and the social.* Oxford, UK: Berg.

Reynolds, A. L., & Baluch, S. (2001). Racial identity in counseling: A literature review and evaluation. In C. L. Wijeyesinghe & B. W. Jackson, III (Eds.), *New perspectives on racial identity development: A theoretical and practical anthology* (pp.153–181). New York, NY: New York University Press.

Ricci et al. v. DeStefano et al., 129 S. Ct. 2658. (2009).

Rockquemore, K. A., & Arend, P. (2003). Opting for white: Choice, fluidity, and racial identity construction in post–civil rights America. *Race and Society, 5*, 49–64.

Rodgers, T., Marshall, E., & Tyson, C. A. (2006). Dialogic narratives of literacy, teaching, and schooling: Preparing literacy teachers for diverse settings. *Reading Research Quarterly, 41*, 202–224.

Roediger, D. R. (1991). *The wages of whiteness: Race and the making of the American working class.* London, UK: Verso.

Roediger, D. R. (1994). *Towards the abolition of whiteness: Essays on race, politics, and working class history.* New York, NY: Verso.

Roediger, D. R. (1997). White looks: Hairy apes, true stories, and Limbaugh's laughs. In M. Hill (Ed.), *Whiteness: A critical reader* (pp. 35–46). New York, NY: New York University Press.

Roediger, D. R. (1998). *Black on white: Black writers on what it means to be white.* New York, NY: Schocken.

Roediger, D. R. (2004). *Chinese immigrants, African-Americans, and racial anxiety in the United States 1848–82.* By Najia Aarim-Heriot. *Journal of Social History, 37*, 802–804.

Rothenberg, P. S. (2004). *White privilege: Essential readings on the other side of racism.* New York, NY: Worth.

Sleeter, C. E. (2001). Epistemological diversity in research on preservice teacher preparation for historically underserved children. *Review of Research in Education, 25*, 209–205.

Sleeter, C. E. (2005). How white teachers construct race. In C. McCarthy, W. Crichlow, G. Dimitriadis, & N. Dolby (Eds.), *Race, identity, and representation in education* (pp. 243–256). New York, NY: Routledge Falmer.

Smedley, A. (1998). "Race" and the construction of human identity. *American Anthropologist, 100*, 690–702.

Solomon, R. O., Portelli, J. P., Daniel, B. J., & Campbell, A. (2005). The discourse of denial: How white teacher candidates construct race, racism, and "white privilege." *Race, ethnicity, and education, 8*, 147–169.

Solórzano, D., & Yosso, T. (2002). Critical race methodology: Counter–storytelling as an analytical framework for education research. *Qualitative Inquiry, 8*(1), 23–44.

Stake, R. E. (1995). *The art of case study research.* Thousand Oaks, CA: Sage.

Stephenson, C. M. (1952). The relation between curriculum entered by white prospective school teachers and their attitudes toward Negroes. *Journal of Educational Sociology, 26*(2), 62–68.

Sue, D. W. (1992, Winter). The challenge of multiculturalism: The road less traveled. *American Counselor, 7*–14.

Sue, D. W. (1993). Confronting ourselves: The white and racial/ethnic minority researcher. *Counseling Psychologist, 21*, 244–249.

Sue, D. W., & Sue, S. (1972). Ethnic minorities: Resistance to being researched. *Professional Psychology, 3*(1), 11–17.

Sue, D. W., & Sue, S. (1999). *Counseling the culturally different: Theory and practice* (3rd ed.). New York, NY: John Wiley & Sons.

Tate, W. (1994). From inner-city to ivory tower: Does my voice matter in the academy? *Urban Education, 29,* 245–269.

Tate, W. (1997). Critical Race Theory and education: History, theory, and implications. *Review of Research in Education, 22,* 195–247.

Tate, W., & Rousseau, C. (2002). Access and opportunity the political and social context of mathematics education. In L. English (Ed.), *Handbook of international research in mathematics education* (pp. 271–299). Mahwah, NJ: Lawrence Erlbaum.

Tatum, B. D. (1994). Teaching white students about racism: The search for white allies and the restoration of hope. *Teachers College Record, 95,* 462–473.

Taylor, E. (2000). Critical race theory and interest convergence in the backlash against affirmative action: Washington State and Initiative 200. *Teachers College Record, 102,* 539–560.

Terry, R. W. (1977). *For white people only.* Grand Rapids, MI: William B. Erdmans.

Tettegah, S. (1996). The racial consciousness attitudes of white prospective teachers and their perceptions of the teachability of students from different racial/ethnic backgrounds: Findings from a California study. *The Journal of Negro Education, 65,* 151–163.

Thompson, A. (2004). Gentlemanly orthodoxy: Critical race feminism, whiteness theory, and the APA manual. *Educational Theory,* 34(1), 27–57.

Thompson, C. E. (2003). Helms's white racial identity development (WRID) theory: Another look. *Counseling Psychologist, 22,* 645–649.

Tierney, W. G. (2003). *Building communities of difference: Higher education in the twenty-first century.* South Hadley, MA: Bergin & Garvey.

Toulmin, S., & Leary, D. E. (1985). The cult of empiricism in psychology and beyond. In S. Kock & D. F. Leary (Eds.), *A century of psychology as science* (pp. 594–617). New York, NY: McGraw-Hill.

Tyson, C. A. (1998). A Response to "Coloring Epistemologies: Are Our Qualitative Research Epistemologies Racially Biased?" *Educational Researcher,* 27(9): 21–22.

Vargas, L. (1999). When the "other" is the teacher: Implications of teacher diversity in higher education. *Urban Review, 31,* 359–383

Watson, L. C., & Watson-Franke, M. (1985). *Interpreting life histories.* New Brunswick, NJ: Rutgers University Press.

West, C. (1990). Black culture and postmodernism. In B. Kreuger & P. Marini (Eds.), *Remaking history* (pp. 87–96). Seattle, WA: Bay Press.

White, H. C. (1992). Cases are for identity, or explanation, or for control. In C. C. Ragin & H. S. Becker (Eds.), *What is a case? Exploring the foundations of social inquiry* (pp. 83–104). Cambridge, UK: Cambridge University Press.

Wieder, A. (2004). Testimony as oral history: Lessons from South Africa. *Educational Researcher, 33*(6), 23–28.

Wiggins, R. A., Follo, E. J., & Eberly, M. B. (2007). The impact of a field immersion program on pre–service teachers' attitudes toward teaching in culturally diverse classrooms. *Teaching and Teacher Education, 23,* 653–663.

Winant, H. (2000). Race and race theory. *Annual Review of Sociology, 26,* 169–185.

Williams, D. G., & Evans-Winter, V. (2005). The burden of teaching teachers: Memoirs of race discourse in teacher education. *Urban Review, 37,* 201–219.

Williams, P. J. (1997). *Seeing a color-blind future: The paradox of race.* New York, NY: Farrar, Straus and Giroux.

Wolcott, H. F. (1983). *Transforming qualitative data: Description, analysis, and interpretation.* Thousand Oaks, CA: Sage.

Wong, P. (2008). Transactions, transformation, and transcendence: Multicultural service-learning experience of preservice teachers. *Multicultural Education, 16*(2), 31–36.

Woods, B. S., & Demerath, P. (2001). A cross–domain exploration of the metaphor "teaching as persuasion." *Theory Into Practice, 40,* 228–234.

Yin, R. K. (1989). *Case study research: Design and methods* (2nd ed.). Newbury Park, CA: Sage.

_____. (2007). Short stuff: The segregation of United States teachers. *Rethinking schools online, 21*(3).

Index

antiracist racism, 99
Bell, Derrick, 7
Black racial identity, 13–14. *See also* Nigrescence. *See also* Racial Identity Development
Bonilla-Silva, Eduardo, 47
circus and research methodology, 29–30
color-blind, 7, 9, 10, 15–16: orientations to race, 47–67, 99; racism, xi, 16, 94; Critical Race Theory, 4, 5; counterstories, 5; expansive and restrictive views of antidiscrimination, 6–7, 48–49; whiteness as property, 4. *See also* semantic moves
Cross, William, 14
diversity as race, 81–85
dysconsiousness, ix, 7, 79, 89, 91, 93, 96, 97, 99, 110, 116
educational debt, 3, 72, 122
Frankenberg, Ruth, 8
Goodenough, Ward, 112
Harris, Cheryl, 5–6
Helms, Janet, 7–10
Helms' Model of White Racial Identity, 100–111: and contact status, 100–102; critiques of, 106–11; disintegration status, 102–3; immersion/emersion status;105–6; pseudo independence, 104–5; reintegration status, 103–4. *See also* white racial identity
Johari's Window, 110–11
Ladson-Billings, Gloria, 3, 4, 122
naïve rationales, 71–80

narratives: incoherent, 88–94; racial, 3; role of, 2; underdeveloped, 88–94
Nigrescence Racial Identity Development, 13–14
Obama, President Barak, ix
phenotype, 13–14
pre-service teachers, literature on, 22–26
prison demographics, 84
propriospect, 112–14, 116
purposive sampling, 33
racial identity: critiques of, 14–15; and counseling, 19–20; and education, 20–21; models, 13–14. *See also* Black racial identity. *See also* white racial identity. *See also* White Racial Identity Development Theory
research methodology: autoethnographic data, role of, 35–36; data analysis, 38–40; epistemologically-centered research, 31–33; interview approach, 35; testimony, 34–35
researcher positionality, 30–31
resegregation, 2, 72
semantic moves, 43–70: and abstract liberalism, 47–49; and color-blind discourse or rhetoric, 7, 9, 10, 16, 41, 47–55, 56–64, 67–70; and conflicts to abstract liberalism, 51–55; and establishment of nonracist expansive standpoints, 49–50; and incoherence, 61–67; and minimalization, 59–61; and naturalization, 56–69; and white racial bonding,

43–46; whiteness as property, 67–
70
student demographics, problem of, 2–3
Supreme Court of the United States:
    *Brown vs. Board of Education of
    Topeka, Kansas*, ix, 47; *Ricci et al.
    vs. DeStefano et al.*, 48–49, 61
Tate, William, 5
Teach for America, xi
teacher demographics: challenges of, 5;
    significance of studying, 10–11
white privilege, 15
white racial identity: color-blind ap-
    proaches to, 15–16, 34, 47–55,
    56–64, 67–70, 94; empirical stud-
    ies in education, 15; edited vol-
    umes on, 21–22; linking to others,
    85–88; new model of, 112–14;
    perspectives on, 16–18; *See also*
    Helms' Model of White Racial
    Identity Development. *See also*
    White Racial Identity Develop-
    ment
White Racial Identity Development
    Theory, 5, 7–10: significance of,
    10–12. *See also* Helms' Model of
    White Racial Identity Develop-
    ment. *See also* white racial identi-
    ty.

About the Author

Kenneth J. Fasching-Varner is an Assistant Professor in Elementary Education and Foundations, as well as the Shirley B. Barton Professor at Louisiana State University. His areas of expertise include educational foundations, pre-service teacher development, reflexive practice, literacy, second-language acquisition and development, multicultural education, Critical Race Theory, and Culturally Relevant Pedagogy. Previously Fasching-Varner was an assistant professor of literacy and bilingual education at Edgewood College in Madison, Wisconsin. Fasching-Varner has a multifaceted research agenda, centered in Critical Race Theory, which examines White racial identity development as it relates to educator identity, culturally relevant engagement, and issues of equity related to schools as a mechanism to work against the school-to-prison pipeline.